My Father's Daughter

Memoir Of A Porn Star

My Father's Daughter
Memoir Of A Porn Star

Copyright © 2014 by Madyson Marquette and Open Sky Publishing
Website: http://madysonmarquette.org

Published by Open Sky Publishing
Castle Rock, Colorado 80109
Website: http://openskypublishing.com

ISBN: 978-0-9826382-5-5

All rights reserved. No part of this publication may be reproduced, stored in a retrieval system, or transmitted in any form buy any means, electronic, mechanical, photocopy, recording or otherwise, without the prior permission of the publisher, except as provided by USA copyright law.

Disclaimer: Names, characters, places and incidents have been changed. Any resemblance to actual events, locales or persons, living or dead, is entirely coincidental.

Scripture quotations are taken from the Holy Bible, New Living Translation, copyright © 1996, 2004. Used by permission of Tyndale House Publishers, Inc., Wheaton, Illinois 60189. All rights reserved.

Cover photo by © Aleshyn Andrei / Shutterstock.com. Used with permission.
Cover and Interior Design by Jason Lohse.

Printed in the United States of America.

My Father's Daughter

Memoir Of A Porn Star

Madyson Marquette

OpenSky
PUBLISHING

DEDICATION

My Father's Daughter is dedicated to the girls I saw lose their lives in the porn industry, and to the ones who continue to fight for their lives and for their freedom.

To my sister "Ava" who understands my pain and for being there for me always.

I also dedicate the book to the very select few that helped me stand up and tell my story, my church, "Zoe", "Grayson" and "Mason" and the ones that stood behind me in some very difficult times.

And last but not least, I dedicate this to my beautiful, adorable son. My prayer is that he will grow up and understand why mommy made the choices she did and that he will grow up knowing the "Real Jesus." I love you doll face.

SPECIAL THANKS

Special thanks to Adam my editor and Clara my proof reader. Thank you Michelle Truax, Esther Fund Project Coordinator at XXXchurch. Thank you Craig Gross founder and director of XXXchurch. Thank you both for all you do, for referring me to my church that had an instrumental part in helping me create this book and for being an extreme light in a very dark world. I would not be where I am now without your ministry. Thank you for teaching me that "Jesus really does love Porn Stars."

Thank you to Nicole Weston at Love146 for taking a stand in the fight against modern-day slavery. Thank you for being there for me. You are very much appreciated.

Thank you to "Peyton" for taking me in when I was scared, afraid and no one else would, even loosing a friendship in order to help me in the process of healing and begin hearing God's voice.

Special thanks to "Mason" for being the first pastor to honor my voice and stand behind me in telling my story. Special thanks to "Grayson" and "Zoe" for also standing behind me in telling my story, for being an instrumental part in getting this book published, and for loving me without condition. Thank you to my church for making my dream a reality. Thank you to my pastors, their wives, and to the people who helped fund this book, making my vision come to life and helping my dream come true. Words will never fully express my gratitude in my heart for you.

Thank you so much to Open Sky Publishing for publishing this book.

Table Of Contents

Making Jesus Happy	11-60
A Broken Heart	61-82
Taken For Granted	83-110
Sheep In Wolves Clothing	111-140
Out Of The Darkness	141-158
Adjusting To Civilian Life	159-182
A Romantic Distraction	183-188
The Real Jesus	189-216

Forward

Madyson Marquette is more than a survivor, more than a fighter, more than an over-comer... she is so much more than her experiences or where they've led her. Madyson holds nothing back as she shares her experiences through almost a decade of work in the porn industry.

This story is not pretty. This story is raw and this story may even shock you as she not only exposes what it was really like behind the camera but also those who seek out the women in it.

This book has the potential to change lives through extraordinary grace, giving hope to those who are exhausted and lost in a lifestyle of sex-industry work. It should also open the eyes of many who are trapped in a stronghold of porn and sex addiction.

Lastly and hopefully it will serve as a wake-up call to the church who thus far, just still doesn't get it.

We have to be willing to get our hands dirty and get right in the 'not-so-pretty' with these people and help them not only find their way out--but discover their dreams and find their purpose. Madyson's life-story shows this doesn't happen overnight but when it does... it's amazing.

It has been an honor for our ministry team to journey with Madyson. She is without a doubt a trophy of God's grace and you will see that for yourself in this book.

Craig Gross
Founder/Director – XXXchurch.com

1

Making Jesus Happy

I grew up in Southern California. Orange County to be exact. I've traveled all over the world, and I still say to this day that Orange County is the one of the most beautiful places on earth. The beaches are absolutely gorgeous; when I go there early in the morning and sit, listening to the waves crashing against the sand, with life peaceful and calm, it is absolute bliss.

I didn't know as I grew up that the beach would become my sanctuary when I needed to get away from the craziness I called life. It was my sweet escape from loud to quiet. For a long time, the quiet scared me, but as I got older, the beach became the one quiet place I felt comfortable.

I had five older sisters, and growing up as the youngest of them definitely gave me a bold fearlessness. I would climb the enormous tree that stood guard in the generous front yard of our single-story white-and-blue home, watch the activity on Beacon Street, and imagine what people's lives might be like. Did they have the fairy tale life I craved?

From my perch, I would see a girl on her bike and imagine her as the princess of a huge castle. Another bike, this time with a boy as its rider, and I would imagine he was a stern-but-kind king. Surely that family driving by was royalty, having a normal dinnertime every night, playing games together, and sleeping peacefully.

I had a big imagination. It and that tree were the only positive things I had. I loved that tree. I talked to it, took care of it, spent hours with it. It was my friend. In some ways, it was my only friend.

Eventually, though, I'd have to shimmy down out of that tree and go through the huge sliding glass door and into the living room. The kitchen was on the left, its bright yellow 1970s cabinets shining with fake cheer. On the left were the three bedrooms. My hell.

My two older sisters (Charlotte and Ava) shared one room; another sister (Avery) and I were in one room, which was decorated with nothing more than our beds, dressers, and some glow-in-the-dark stars stuck on the ceiling. I was so proud of those stars. They became another place for my imagination, where I could go when I was scared or did not want to think about what was happening to me.

The last room was for my parents. Except they didn't share it—my father slept every night on the blue couch in our living room.

We had two more sisters (Bella and Sophie) who were much older than me and didn't live with us—I think they desperately wanted to get out of that house as early as they could, just like I did. Bella married her high-school sweetheart, Samuel, at nineteen and never looked back. Sophie was thirteen years older than me and independent; she was flashy and crazy and comfortably her own person, and I looked up to her in just about every way.

I do have some happy memories from childhood: one is riding my bike down to the park and playing with my sisters, especially my sister Ava. She's always been a true sister and the only one in my life who understands how deep my pain is, how much I suffered at the hand of my father and mother—because she experienced it just as I did. It is our unspoken truth and our strongest bond.

Some of my best memories, though, are of a time when my sisters and I would do a show called Fashion of Each Era. See, Sophie had a friend named Peyton who often had "visions" of ministry, which Sophie would make into a reality. She was just good at it.

One particular vision of Peyton's was a fashion show, a "trend from beginning to end." It began with Adam and Eve running down the catwalk, and then presented fashions from the beginning of time all the way up to the 1990s with a gospel presentation at the end. Well, who better for Sophie to recruit for models than her own sisters? Ava and I readily agreed—for me it was a dream come true. I mean for my oldest sister to think I was pretty enough to be in a Fashion Show? Of course I said yes.

I was in scenes from the 1920s, 1950s, 1970s, and 1990s; after each era there was a short message and then, at the end of the show, one of Sophie's friends (usually Peyton) gave a gospel message while a singer named Crystal Lewis sang a song called "Come Just As You Are." I loved that song, especially the beautiful way Crystal sang it with her amazing voice. I didn't know then that very song would save me from trying to kill myself years later. I also didn't know that Crystal and the person who wrote it would be such a huge piece of my future.

I loved doing these shows. I held on to those memories through many dark times, and part of the reason why was Peyton. A gifted speaker with short, blonde, frazzled hair, Peyton always had her Bible with her, and you could tell she read it because it was falling apart at the seams. She loved me, and while I don't know if it was because I was Sophie's sister or because God had given her a heart for me at a young age, when I grew up, she would be the one there for me, taking me in broken and afraid. I saw the real Jesus in Peyton; I just didn't know until I was in my thirties what or who that was.

My less fond childhood memories are of my mother and father. As the sixth child, I always felt like the forgotten one. People say the baby is supposed to get attention and be spoiled, but I wasn't, and when I wanted to talk with my mom she couldn't be bothered; she would shoo me away, or she would tell my sister to let me watch Duck Tales so she didn't have to talk to me. She wanted peace and I wasn't giving her that—I was a little girl that wanted her mother. My mother was also too busy finally obtaining her education in her late thirties to be bothered with me.

My father? Well, he was just a pure creep. He was a child molester and a rapist. But he was a great actor. My father was tall with black hair and brown eyes, with a thin frame and a little pot belly. He had a sweet face, so no one ever imagined him to be a "bad man;" he was just a father of six girls. People would pity him for that, saying, "Poor guy; he never had any sons." I never thought he wanted boys, because he had girls to touch and betray. I'm kind of glad I didn't have brothers; if he had sons, would my father have had them do the same thing to me that he was doing?

I remember the first time. My father stalked into my room quietly one night. "What is about to happen is God's will," he said. "You want to make Jesus happy, don't you?"

You ask a little girl who believes in Jesus whether she wants to make him happy, and of course he answer is going to be yes. "Yes, Daddy," I said. "I want to make Jesus happy."

"Take off your clothes."

I looked up with complete innocence. "Why do I need to do that?"

"Do you want to make Jesus happy?" he repeated more strongly.

"Yes."

"Then take off your clothes."

So I did.

That night started many nights of rape, molestation, and abuse that are still so horrific that even writing about them is difficult. I was young and thought what my father was doing was normal. Every night when the house fell so silent you could hear everyone's deep breathing while they slept, my father would come into my room, bend down, and ask me the same question:

"Do you want to make Jesus happy?"

After that first night, I didn't say anything. I just took my clothes off.

He would take off his clothes, push my long blonde hair out of my face and caress my face with the back of his hand like he was making love to me—while raping me and making me do things to him. That caress still hurts. To this day, I struggle with caressing my own son's face, even though I touch him in a pure way to show him my affection, to express the love that runs so deep between me and him. It is such a pure, innocent act turned into something so evil by my father.

Over time, after repeated abuse, I wanted to scream a reply: No! I don't want to make Jesus happy anymore! I hate Jesus! I hate you! Leave me alone! But night after night, I stayed silent and instead got lost in the glow-in-the-dark stars on my ceiling.

I shared that room with my sister Avery, who was only eighteen months older than me. Avery grew very tall and beautiful, carrying herself with the same confidence that Sophie did. Avery had short brown hair and brown eyes and was very skinny and put-together, like a prep school student. She and I never really got along, and though I can't really tell you why, I have some ideas. Maybe she resented me for being born and replacing her as the youngest, or maybe it was just sibling rivalry since we were so close in age.

Or maybe she just felt a sense of guilt, because she was always in the room when my father did what he did to me. Maybe she felt bad about not doing something to stop it. Maybe she felt relieved it wasn't happening to her—and then felt guilt about that relief. However she felt, I didn't blame her. I just went to my stars.

† † †

The day I got those stars was one of the best days of my then-young life. I loved science and bought them at the science store in the Westminster Mall. When I got home, Avery helped me put them on the ceiling correctly so they were accurate and looked just like the sky outside. Avery knew I wanted those stars to get lost in, and I think a part of her wanted to get lost in them, too. She would hear my father molesting and raping me; she would hear me crying every night. Maybe she could see the tears run down my face as my father climbed off me. My father didn't care when I cried—I think he liked it more, honestly. It added to the thrill.

When I cried, he got more aggressive, so I learned very quickly to control my emotions and not to cry until after he was done. He loved making sure I suffered at his hand. What I didn't understand—and still don't—is that I was his baby, his little girl, and yet he touched me in places no little girl should be touched at my age; he stole from me an innocence I could never get back and manipulated me in a way no father should. This was supposed to be my daddy, but my daddy hurt me every night.

Every night after he was done, I would get up and go into the bathroom and scrub my body so hard that sometimes I would make myself bleed. I couldn't get clean enough.

I don't know if he ever did anything to my sisters, because whenever I tried to ask them they would not talk about it. People used to tell me I had an innocence about me, and I think that was true for a while. The older I got, however, the more that innocence slowly deteriorated; I got angrier and angrier about the things that were happening to me. I was angry because my mom would not stand up and protect me: Why didn't she tell him to stop? Why didn't she call the police? Why did she stay in her room while her husband raped and molested her youngest daughter? I wanted my mom to love me enough to protect me, but she just let it happen. She didn't physically rape me, but she became an accomplice through inaction.

I was so angry at so many things. I was angry because my sisters didn't protect me—they just moved out and left. Bella was married, Sophie only came and went until she eventually got married. Charlotte and Ava were teenagers getting ready for college, with jobs and friends, so they were never home; they eventually left and went to college out of state. Avery would never talk to me. I felt like my sisters left me to rot in a home with a broken mother and a sadistic father. I don't blame my sisters now, but I did then.

Of course I went from being innocent to confused to angry, eventually hating my family, life, God, and everything I was. I was a little girl who, day by day, learned how to survive. So I sought peace in the stars at night. During the day, I climbed up in my tree.

I used to talk to the tree and tell it how angry I was at what my daddy was doing and how angry I was that my mommy wasn't doing anything about it. I know now that Jesus was sitting in that tree with me, but I didn't know that when I was a little girl; after all, I was being told the only way to make Jesus happy was to let my father take advantage of me.

As the years went by, I became a teenager who was like a caged lion waiting to come out. I started finding the easiest ways possible to get away from my parents, like spending the night at friends' houses whenever I could. I began to realize what was happening to me wasn't normal.

† † †

When I was sixteen, I began spending a lot of time with a friend named Grace. She was a year older than me, with long black hair and brown eyes. We went to school together at Baptist Church and School, a small private academy operated by the church my family attended, and where my mother worked. Our school was so small that age differences didn't matter and everyone just hung out with everyone; Grace accepted me as a peer and we hit it off.

I began to stay at Grace's house as much as I could to get away from the nightmare I called my life, from the helplessness and loneliness I felt by being at home. Grace's family described themselves as "apostolic," and she asked me one day if I wanted to go to church with her. I used to tell Grace that my parents would fight all the time, but I never told her what my father was doing; I think Grace knew I was searching for an escape, thus the invite.

Her church was called "Iglesia," and they had services every Tuesday, Thursday, and Sunday, which created even more opportunities for me to get out of my house and spend time with my friend. The funny part, though, was that all the church services were in Spanish. Here I was, this sixteen-year-old white girl with blonde hair and hazel eyes, attending an all-Spanish church. (I didn't mind—I eventually became fluent!). But even though it was in Spanish and I didn't understand most of what was being said, I felt somewhat of a peace there. Even though this church had people running down the aisles, speaking in tongues, and doing flips off the podium, there was a sense of calm about it. Because they were not hurting anyone. They were searching for something; in the midst of their craziness they sought a purpose.

I think everyone in life wants a purpose—this church and the people in it, had something that made them peaceful, and I wanted to know who their Jesus was. My Jesus was my father telling me rape was okay. My Jesus wasn't there for me. My Jesus abandoned me as a little girl.

My Jesus was evil.

Their Jesus was love, and peace, and acceptance. Yes, they were a little crazy, but their Jesus had to be better than the one I knew. I was searching for something to help me be complete and I thought this church had it, because everyone who went there seemed to be complete. All the hermanas (sisters) were sweet to me every time I went, affectionately telling me I was too skinny and needed to eat, but still accepting me for me.

One Tuesday night at Iglesia, I looked up and there was this boy with wavy hair playing the bass. He looked back at me a couple times, we smiled at each other, and that was it—I had fallen for him. I went back Grace's house and told her I thought this boy was so cute and I had a crush on him. Maybe I liked him because he was playing in the church band or because he had a nice smile. When he was playing the bass, all I noticed was him—people were running up and down the aisles speaking in tongues, but he was all I could see.

"That's the pastor's son!" Grace said.

I laughed. "Well, forget that!" I said. A pastor's son falling in love with a girl like me, who was raped by her father every night she was home? No way.

I continued attending church with Grace and started to get to know some of the people there. One woman was kind of heavyset, always had a smile on her face, and was always dressed to the nines. Grace introduced me one night: "This is the pastor's wife, Evelyn."

Evelyn gave me the biggest, most genuine hug I had ever received. My mom never touched me or hugged me or told me she loved me, so when Evelyn hugged me it was the first time that a woman who was a "mother figure" had actually done so. I guess even as a teenager I continued to crave a mother figure because my mother had never been much of one. I wanted my mom to hug me and tell me everything was going to be okay—but she never did. I fell into that hug from Evelyn.

I got to know the pastor and his family very well, which means I got to know their bass-playing son. His name was Carter. I loved being with them. They represented what a normal family was supposed to be: loving and caring.

I was at dinner with them one night when Evelyn shocked me. She said, "We really like you and think you should date Carter."

I didn't know what to say. I was just dazed. So I looked over at Carter...

"Will you be my girlfriend?" he said.

I had never had a boyfriend before. There were only a few boys at my school and I'd never looked at any of them like that.

Carter could be someone I could talk about while I was at school; I could tell everyone about my cool, pastor's-son boyfriend, Carter.

"Yes," I said.

"Great!" Evelyn said. "We'll talk about you getting baptized, too."

I really didn't know what that meant, so I agreed to being baptized.

Carter and I started to date and I spent more and more time with him and his family, going to every church event they had, every service. I felt happy for the first time in a long time.

I still lived with my parents, and in the midst of my frequent escapes, my home life became worse and worse. As I grew into more of a woman, my father wanted me more, and my mother still refused to stop it. But things got worse for me, because I started to become a fighter. See, I wasn't this little girl anymore—I was a teenager who had a lot of spirit. My father didn't like fighting me, and my mother hated hearing me, so along with being raped and molested, I was now being beaten into quiet submission. My father liked seeing the pain in my eyes.

When I was a little girl, I wouldn't scream; but now I did. "I don't want to make Jesus happy!" I would scream. I hated Jesus,

I hated everyone in the house, I hated my mother and father, so I screamed. I screamed for help, but none came.

I was desperate to just be a normal teenage girl with a normal boyfriend. No one knew I was being abused, because our school dress code required wearing long skirts that covered my legs and long sleeves, and the style of dress at Iglesia was similar, so all my bruises were completely covered.

† † †

During all this, my mom had a major mental breakdown. She kept telling me to take this karate elective at school, and though I didn't want to, I enrolled in it just to get her off my back. The teacher was a kind, blonde, blue-eyed man named Mr. Wyatt, and his daughter Brooklyn helped him in class. Mr. Wyatt was a nice man—he seemed kind and gentle; he didn't seem scary like my father. When Mr. Wyatt spoke, you would listen because he was a man of few words.

He always paid special attention to my karate technique, and I never knew why until my mother sat down with me one day and said something very out of the ordinary. "Madyson," she said,

"I want you to think of Mr. Wyatt like a father. If you need anything, you can go to him."

My first thought was, This lady has lost it. My second thought was, Is this guy going to rape me, too? That's what I thought fathers did.

Mr. Wyatt never hurt me in any way, though; his only mistake was falling in love with my mother. Turns out she was having an affair with him, which my mother justified because my father was having an affair. She didn't tell me who my father was having an affair with, and she said it matter-of-factly, like it was something I already knew.

Eventually Mr. Wyatt got fired from the school, for a reason I am unsure of. My mom tried desperately to keep her relationship going, so she let Brooklyn come live with us. Brooklyn was tall and gorgeous, with long blonde hair and really light eyes. She lived with us for so long she practically became our sister, though I still to this day don't know why Mr. Wyatt couldn't take care of her or what happened to her mother. All I knew is Brooklyn lived with us and became part of our family.

As the length of time Brooklyn lived with us grew longer, I sometimes wondered: Was she scared? Is this house really better than her parents' house? Was her life so bad that living with us was an improvement? These questions were in the background, though, because I loved Brooklyn and always wanted to be around her. Maybe a part of me craved her company because I felt she was broken and lost just like me, and I wanted to be around someone on the outside who might understand what I was going through.

Brooklyn used to make fun of me for being in the apostolic church. "You only go there for the boy," she said. "You won't be apostolic when you grow up."

She was right. I grew up to be a porn star.

After some time, Brooklyn got married and moved out. My mother's relationship with Mr. Wyatt was over, and she and my father decided to go to marriage counseling at the Baptist church I'd grown up in. But it seemed like after each counseling session, my parents would come home to scream and yell at one another. Their anger was extremely intense.

My mother would yell at my father about having an affair with a Hispanic lady; my father would yell at my mother about having an affair with Henry, their marriage counselor and pastor of the church (and headmaster of my school). Then they would find whatever they could to throw at each other, saying how much they hated each other and how they wished the other would die.

They would also yell about having six girls, and how having that many kids ruined their lives. When this happened, whichever sisters were home and I would go into one room together, curl up on a single bed, and fall asleep. It was probably the only time in our childhood when we all got along.

† † †

In the midst of all this craziness, my mother got promoted, becoming the principal of the elementary school while I was finishing out high school. My mother also began to get quite upset that I was going to the apostolic church. It was really weird; one minute she did not care where I went, then suddenly it was as if people from Iglesia church were the devil, so she insisted I stop going.

I was devastated. This church was my escape; it was my happiness. I tried to reason with her. I told her a lot of other kids are out drinking, smoking, and doing drugs—I was going to church three times a week.

My mother didn't care, because in the midst of her counseling, she had begun a romantic and physical relationship with the pastor of the baptist church, Henry. It wasn't the first time

Pastor Henry had done something like that; he counseled many women at their weakest point, when they needed just a little bit of love and attention, and preyed on that. He counseled them, then slept with them.

And now he was doing the same thing with my mother, becoming so controlling of her that he now wanted to control me. He hated that I went to the apostolic church. He called it a cult. It also didn't look right that the elementary school principal's daughter didn't want to go to Pastor Henry's church every Sunday. It wasn't good for his image.

Every morning at school, we started with Bible class. One morning, I was pulled out of this class and called to the pastor's office. As I sat in the waiting room, I began to stew in my emotions, all the hate, anger, and rage I felt towards Henry. I hated my father, but I also hated Henry for causing the fights my parents had. He was supposed to help my parents and he made it worse.

Pastor Henry came in with his bald little head and his mousy voice. "How are you doing?" he asked.

I didn't say a word. I just looked at him.

"How is school going?"

Again I looked at him and did not say anything. Instead I just wondered, How does he get his head so shiny? I wanted him to tell me what he was going to tell me and then let me leave.

"I've been talking to your mother about all your issues," he said.

I finally spoke. "What issues are those?"

"That you're running around with a boy in a cult," he said. "You aren't acting like a proper lady. I think of you like my daughter, and I want you to stop going to that church."

Why do all these men think they have to be my father? I thought. Was my mother trying to find me a new one because she allowed the one I had to hurt me night after night?

"Absolutely not," I said.

Then Pastor Henry said something I will never forget. He leaned forward with an arrogant smirk on his face like what he was about to say was coming directly from God's mouth. "Okay, let me put it like this: I am your father, and as the pastor and leader of this church, I demand you stop going to this apostolic church!"

I looked back at him with defiance. "What are you going to do if I don't?"

"I'm not going to allow you to graduate high school, and I'm going to kick you off the basketball and volleyball teams."

"You can't do that," I said.

"Oh, but I can."

Burning with rage, all my hatred came pouring out. I looked Pastor Henry right in the eye and said, "You little motherf***er. I know you're sleeping with my mom, but you are not my father and you never will be. If going to church is going to get me kicked out of school, then goodbye!"

As I stood up, I saw a glass cross on his desk. I snatched it up and threw it on the floor as I stormed out, hearing it shatter into pieces behind me. I immediately strode through the chapel toward my mother's office, but she met me halfway, grabbed me, threw me up against the wall, and said, "You little brat! You will not go to that apostolic church anymore! You will do what Pastor Henry tells you!"

As she repeatedly slammed me against the wall and hit me, I felt a power come over me. I was sick of being beaten up, I was sick of being abused. I pushed her back and, as she raised her hand again, I grabbed it, ready to clock her one.

As all this was happening, a teacher named David showed up and restrained my mother. "Don't touch her!" he said to her. It was the first time anyone had stuck up for me, the first time someone actually cared about what was happening to me.

I looked at David with thankful eyes and ran home.

Our house was not far from the school, maybe ten minutes on foot or three minutes driving, so I was home quickly. My mother came home about an hour later and continued the abuse, throwing all sorts of objects at me.

"You're an ungrateful little brat!" she said. "You were a mistake, anyway! I went into the hospital to have my tubes tied and found out I was pregnant with you! I should have had an abortion!" She said over and over how much I was the one who ruined her life and messed up everything.

I was just a kid, a teenager, and my mother couldn't just hug me and tell me she was sorry for things that had happened. She turned it around on me. She was angry I didn't listen to her, angry that I actually was fighting back.

"I don't care if you hate me!" I said. "You raped me too for not stopping it! You're a rapist!" Then I fell to the floor and sobbed and sobbed.

My mother knelt close to my ear and whispered, "Your tears don't work on me." Then she slapped me. She grabbed my arms and beat me, creating bruises up and down my arm.

She finally stopped after about an hour and left. I didn't know where she went, and I didn't care. I just couldn't take any of the abuse anymore so that night, as my mother and father screamed at each other in their room, I snuck out and ran away. I didn't have anywhere to go, so I ran to the liquor store down the street. When I was younger, I used to ride my bike there to get candy, so the manager knew me.

"Can I use your phone?" I asked. He agreed and I called Bella, who was married, with her own apartment, and I told her everything that had taken place that day.

"I'm coming," she said.

While I waited for her to show up, I hid behind the candy rack and shook with fear and nervousness, afraid my parents would notice I was missing and come find me.

After I was with Bella, she called my mother to inform her I was okay. My mother also called Sophie, and then, for some reason, called everyone from church and school, including the youth pastor Max (who was Pastor Henry's son-in-law), Pastor Henry, and my father. They all showed up at Bella's apartment.

My mother was livid. "You're kidnapping her!" she said to Sophie and Bella. "Hand her over!"

"Just let her spend the night here," Bella said, "and then we can talk in the morning."

"I'm going to call the police," my mother said. And she did.

A few minutes later, four separate police cars arrived, so the officers separated everyone and took me off to the side to ask me what happened. Unfortunately, I was so shaken up I couldn't tell them anything in detail. One of the officers noticed the bruises on my arm, though. "Do you want to go home?" he said. "Or would you rather stay with your sisters?"

"Please let me stay with my sisters," I said.

The police calmed my mother down and asked her if it was okay if I spent the night with one of my sisters.

"Madyson can stay with them tonight," she said, "but she has to come home tomorrow."

So, that's what happened. I spent the night with Bella and went home the next day, terrified of what might happen since my mom had been so out of control the night before.

And yet, when I got home, I realized I was done being scared. I was done showing my mother and father that I was afraid of them, so when I got home, I told my mother I was not going to stop going to the apostolic church.

"Fine," she said, "but you can't go to school anymore. You won't graduate and you can't be around any of your friends. You're choosing the church over your education."

I was so upset, but I just thought, Fine, I don't care.

† † †

A few days later, a strange man and woman showed up at my house. The woman was wearing a pantsuit and the man was wearing a regular suit, and they seemed really scary and stern, like they were undercover police officers. They asked to speak with my mother. They took my mother outside and kept her out there for a long time before coming back into the house and separating me and my sister Avery. They took Avery into our room and told me to sit down on the blue couch in our living room. I did.

They questioned us individually about the night when my mom beat me up. They looked at my arm and asked about my bruises, but I didn't say anything to them since I didn't know who they were.

The woman got really close to my face. "Little girl, do you know where I work?"

"No," I said.

"I work for social services," she said, "and I don't think there's really a problem in this household, so you're going to tell my partner everything is okay." She leaned even closer. "You know

I can put you in a really bad house with really bad people, and I guarantee you don't want us to do that to you."

I was so scared that I said whatever this lady wanted me to say. I painted my mother as Mother Teresa and my father as a hero... I made them out to be the complete opposite of what they really were.

It turned out that my mother had paid this woman off so she wouldn't look bad. My mother's job was at risk. I mean, imagine if the principal of an elementary school got her kids taken away and was accused of being an abuser—now that would be a scandal.

So nothing happened.

Eventually, my mother kicked my father out. I don't know what her breaking point was; maybe she just wanted to have the freedom to have her love affair, or maybe she was done with their marriage. I don't know, I just know she told him to never come back. So he left, and he didn't come back.

I was relieved, because my father's absence meant that when I went to sleep at night I could actually sleep with no fear that he would appear. I had nightmares, but if I woke up, I still had those glow-in-the-dark stars on my ceiling to help me. I never took them down.

I continued to go the apostolic church, which caused a lot of problems with my mother, but even as my relationship with my mother suffered, I started to get closer with my oldest sister, Sophie. She is thirteen years my elder, and I looked up to her so much. I loved her. I wanted to be like her.

She began to tell me things that our mother had said and done to her when she was a little girl, things that were similar to what I had been enduring. See, Sophie was the first mistake, because my mother had gotten pregnant with her at fifteen, while I was the last mistake, because I was never supposed to be conceived. Sophie and I began spending more and more time together, and I think she tried to step into the role of a mother for me. She knew I needed someone, because she had no one when she was my age.

My mother, on the other hand, had finally grown fed up with me and kicked me out of her house. I was sixteen years old. I think she was tired and didn't want to be a mom anymore—and I'm sure Pastor Henry had a lot to do with the decision, too.

Anytime my mother and I would get in a fight, I would call her a cheater and tell her I hated her. I did hate her—she stole my childhood just as my father did—but I knew saying those things wasn't right. But how could I not be angry?

Either way I was kicked out of my house, unable to graduate from high school, so I needed a place to live.

† † †

I went to Evelyn and told her I had nowhere to go, and of course she came to my rescue. She found a Hispanic family to take me into their house, and they let me have a few months to find a job before beginning to pay them rent at three hundred dollars a month. It was a married couple with a little girl who was four and a little boy who was seven. It was kind of hilarious since the adults spoke no English and I didn't yet know Spanish. For a long time the seven-year-old translated, but eventually this family taught me Spanish and I taught them English.

I soon found a job as a stock girl at Nordstrom, working from six a.m. to three p.m. I didn't have a car, so I walked about fifteen minutes to and from work every day, carrying a lunch that the mother of this family made for me. She woke up early every morning to have that lunch ready for me when I walked out the door. Such generosity.

Every day when I got home from work, I immediately went to my room. I was an uncomfortable and lost kid living with a family

I didn't know who didn't speak my language. It was like living in a foreign country. Even though I'd come out of a worse situation with my family, I felt so alone in this house despite their efforts to make me feel welcome. I was dealing with major rejection at the age of sixteen and didn't know until I was older what that truly meant.

Eventually, though, I became close with the couple and their kids, mainly through sheer force of their will. I would come home and try to go to my room, but the kids wanted me to play and ride bikes with them, or teach them English. The more time I spent with them, the more I came to love these kids, and I started to love the family.

It was the first time in my life I wasn't being hurt and I wasn't being abused. At certain times throughout my life, God has made sure His light was known, even if I didn't know it. This was one of those times; this family simply loved me without even knowing me. That was Jesus.

After about a year, this family moved away, and I needed to find a new place to live. Sophie asked me to move in with her. At the time, she didn't live far from where this family lived, so I could still work at Nordstrom. I know Sophie really had good intentions, but I think along the way things got twisted because she wanted to defeat my mom in some sort of love competition, and having me on her side did just that.

Sophie hated my mother and though I didn't really know the specifics, I knew why I hated my mother—for not protecting me from my father—and wondered if Sophie hated her for the same reason. Sophie did take me under her wing; she knew I was being diligent in walking to work every day, so she decided to help me get a car—a Volkswagen Rabbit convertible wagon. If you don't know what that car is, then you know exactly how old it is.

Things went really well for a while living with Sophie; I had a boyfriend, a car and a job at the sophisticated age of seventeen. I was an adult. I was excited to move in with Sophie and her husband Aiden. I was excited because, as a little girl, I had heard all about her adventures, and I guess a part of me thought I would get to experience a little bit of that with her, not realizing she was now a grown woman, a wife with real-life responsibilities. She was no longer a twenty-year-old who could pick up and go.

† † †

Once I was all moved in, I continued to go to the apostolic church, and Sophie never said anything about it. I was still dating

Carter, so that meant I needed to follow the rules of the apostolic church and get baptized "in Jesus' name" in order to stay with my boyfriend. They believed that you are saved through being baptized in Jesus' name and then speaking in tongues; once you have done this, you are truly saved.

I knew I needed to get baptized to be saved, but I didn't know what that meant at the time. I was just a teenager who wanted to keep her boyfriend, and if that meant getting dunked underwater, then that's what I would do.

I invited my mother to my baptism, but she wanted nothing to do with me. It's amazing how a little girl still craves approval from a mother who was unstable, dysfunctional, and abusive. I wanted a mother who didn't want me.

When Sophie heard this, she said, "Don't worry about it. Mom will never be there for you; you should just cut her out of your life. The pain isn't worth it."

But I still wanted my mom. I was only a kid. And it's strange to realize that now, as I write this, neither Sophie nor my mother is in my life. Still, Sophie and her husband agreed to come see me baptized, and I could not have been more thrilled to have some family there. Of course, they stood out like a sore thumb, just like I did. There they were, my sister in her ripped jeans and Aiden dressed just as casually, seated next to these women with their long skirts, long hair, and veils on top of their heads running up and down the aisles.

Again, I did not really know what it meant to get baptized. Evelyn and her husband Declan told me that if I didn't get baptized in Jesus' name I would not go to heaven, but all I knew about being baptized was that you get in this big tank of water, get dunked, and come back up. Who would have thought that something I did easily as a teenager would become my biggest fear in my thirties? (Keep reading; we'll get to that.)

Grace's father actually baptized me; because he had known me since I was a little girl, he was considered the "appropriate" person to baptize me.

As I waited to get baptized, I looked out into the crowd to see if Sophie and Aiden had arrived yet and saw them in the very back row of the pews. The church wasn't very big, so it was probably about eight rows back. When I saw them I immediately smiled, but my smile turned to complete horror when I saw my father sitting next to them.

I had a sinking feeling in my stomach. I did not want him there. I wanted to scream at him, "Leave! Get out! I hate you!" but I couldn't—I just sat in my seat waiting for them to call my name.

When they did, I walked from the front row to a room that led to the baptismal. Evelyn was standing there to help me, handing me a white robe to wear. I stepped into the water, and Grace's dad baptized me in the name of Jesus in both Spanish and English.

I still didn't understand what being baptized meant. Evelyn had just told me it was a requirement to get into heaven, but even in the moment, excited that I was being baptized and that Sophie and Aiden were there, I didn't care if I went to heaven.

I was angry at God, though I never told anyone… I was good at playing the part of acting like everything was okay. But internally, I continued to question God. Why? Why did you give me the mother and father I had? Why did you let my father do that? I never said these things aloud to anyone; I just kept it in.

Carter and I spent even more time together after my baptism, becoming best friends. We dated for three years while I worked at Nordstrom and stayed with Sophie, and things really started to become normal in my life. I wasn't scared my dad was going to come into my room. I wasn't scared my parents would scream and throw things at each other. I wasn't scared of Aiden because he just wasn't scary—he was patient and kind to me, and he was graciously allowing me to live with him and my sister in their new marriage.

† † †

I eventually decided to see if I could get an office job, so I started applying and eventually got a call to work in the call center of a large software company called Sage Software. It was a nice change, and it gave me an opportunity to learn something new. I caught on very quickly and discovered I was good at the computer part of the job.

Sage had a university of sorts where employees could become software technicians, so I enrolled and started going to the school twice a week at night. It was nice to learn something new, but it felt especially fulfilling to go to school and receive a certificate for a job since I didn't get my high school diploma. It was an amazing feeling.

When I started working at Sage, I became much more mature, a process I'd really already begun as a young child. Carter was still in high school, about to graduate and go to college, but he wasn't really growing up. I had to grow up and become responsible in order to be on my own, but Carter was able to be a normal teenager. He also started getting extremely jealous that I was working, accusing me of cheating on him no matter how much I assured him I was being faithful and that I was just trying to move up in my career.

He didn't believe it. He wanted me to be available to him all day, every day, and my schedule didn't allow that. Our relationship began to spiral out of control, and Carter became more aggressive with me.

During the tragic events of September 11, 2001, I was driving to work, and Carter kept trying to call me. He couldn't get through because all cell phones were down, and when he tried to call my office, he couldn't get through because our corporate office was in the World Trade Center. I didn't know what was going on until I got to work.

There was chaos and crying, and we all just did what we could to make it through the day. Carter tried to call me all day and when he couldn't get through, he finally decided at the end of the day to drive up to my office. I was supposed to have class that night, and our professor decided to go on with it—maybe so no one had to go home and be alone, or maybe because he didn't want to be alone.

As I sat at my desk waiting for class to start, I heard someone call my name and looked up to see Carter standing in front of my desk.

"How did you get in the building?" I asked. It was a logical question: the doors automatically locked at night for security.

He didn't answer me; he just grabbed my arm and said, "Let's go. I've been calling you all day."

I jerked my arm back. "You need to leave," I said. "I have class and I don't want to get fired for having my boyfriend in my office building after hours."

He was so mad that he took my arm back and gripped it really hard. "If you don't come to my house after work, you're going to be sorry."

"Okay, okay," I said, waiting for him to let go.

I sat through class in a daze—this world-changing event had just happened and the guy who was supposed to love me just risked my job and livelihood. It was a lot to process.

I went to Carter's house that night after work, and he was so angry, yelling at me for not contacting him. His parents had ordered pizza for everyone, and he was so mad he picked up a still-hot pizza and threw it at his mother and me; we both ducked and it hit their refrigerator. I was so shocked I stood in their kitchen next to the refrigerator, staring in disbelief.

"Sweetheart," Evelyn said in Spanish, "Why don't you leave, Carter is too upset right now."

"You can't leave!" Carter yelled. "If you do, you'll be sorry!"

Pastor Declan, Carter's father, intervened. He turned to me and, using the Spanish affectation for daughter, said, "Mija, you can leave." Then he turned to Carter and began yelling at him in rapid Spanish.

I didn't stick around to try to translate; I just got out of there and drove home. It seemed like the longest drive ever, and when I got home I sat in my car and replayed the day and night over and over in my head, trying to get my mind around it. I was grateful to put it behind me when I went to bed that night.

The next day was our four-year anniversary. We had been together three years officially, but the year before I got baptized we'd hung out quite a bit, so we were celebrating four years of being friends, falling in love, and growing up. We had plans to meet at Nordstrom at the mall where I used to work, but I did not want to go. Maybe my reluctance was because I'd grown up more than he had, or maybe I was done with his verbal abuse and just couldn't get over the night before.

Carter called me all morning and left messages begging me to come meet him, and I finally relented, agreeing to meet and go to the mall. We took my car, though he drove, and once we were on our way, he apologized repeatedly until I interrupted him.

"Carter, I don't want to do this anymore," I said. "You're risking my job and my future."

He got so mad that he opened the door and pushed me out of the still-moving car.

I tucked into a ball, scraping up my entire leg, feet, and hands as I rolled. Luckily, nothing was broken. Dazed, I just lay there in the road and thought, What would it hurt if I were run over right now and killed?

Carter pulled over, came and got me, apologized, and then acted like it was no big deal. We then drove to the mall and sat in the parking lot to gather ourselves. I told him to switch seats with me; maybe my intuition told me I should have control of something in this situation.

After we switched I picked up where I'd left off. "Carter," I said, "I just don't want to be with you anymore."

He started to cry. "I was going to propose to you today," he said. "We are supposed to get married."

Married? I thought, That's the last thing I want!

"I can't be with you," I said. "We need to break up."

Once I said those words, something glossed over Carter's face and he was no longer the same person I had fallen in love with years earlier. He looked like something had possessed him, and it scared me. He then looked at me and head-butted me right in the nose.

Immediately my nose started gushing out blood, and I jumped out of the car.

"Enough is enough," I said, managing to remain calm. "If you do not get out of this car, I am going to start screaming at the top of my lungs."

He was mortified at his actions and began saying, "I'm sorry, I'm sorry." He got out and closed the door; I jumped in and drove off. I went straight to his aunt's house because she and I were close and I knew it would be a safe place.

† † †

When I arrived, Carter's aunt, Dolores, told me to go to the hospital and call the police. So that's what I did. While driving to the hospital I called Rick, my sister Charlotte's husband, who was a member of the California Highway Patrol. He met me at the hospital right away and helped me fill out a police report, then called Charlotte, as well as Sophie and Aiden.

Someone, I don't know who, called my mother, and she quickly showed up at the hospital. In the midst of all the police and doctors, I kept looking at my mom. I wanted to just fall into her arms and cry, but I knew I couldn't. She wasn't there for me; she just wanted a front row seat to the drama so she could go tell everyone how horrible things were for her.

There was already so much commotion with people asking me questions and poking and prodding me, that my mother's presence was the last straw. I had a nervous breakdown and started yelling for everyone to get out of the room.

"Get out!" I screamed. "I just want to go home!"

The doctor began to usher everyone out, but I interrupted him.

"Sophie," I said, "will you stay with me?"

She nodded.

"I'm staying, too," Charlotte said, which was fine with me. I just didn't want to see my mom. Rick stayed in the room, too, but everyone else left.

After all the tests, the doctors let me know my nose was broken and I had a sprained ankle from being pushed out of the car, but the injuries didn't require me to stay overnight in the hospital, so they discharged me.

I figured everyone would be going to Sophie's house to talk about what just happened, and since I just wanted to go to sleep, I called Dolores and asked if I could come over. She told me to come spend the night.

It seemed like something was right about being with her, maybe because her house was quiet. There was a peace there—you could tell she and her husband loved each other, and I think because I felt that love between them, I felt the same peace in their house that they did. I'd been around Dolores a lot while Carter and I dated, and she always loved me without condition.

†　†　†

After that night, I went back to Sophie's house, but we weren't there long. Sophie and Aiden were moving to Hollywood to start a church, and so I moved with them. Where else was I going to go?

We lived on Sunset Boulevard on the strip; right outside their apartment were prostitutes and homeless people, and though I didn't know it then, I would eventually become one of those prostitutes.

I continued to commute to my job for a little while, but it wasn't long until they fired me for Carter coming in without authorization. Meanwhile, living with Sophie and Aiden started to become a little more difficult, because they wanted to act like my parents and I was a legal adult.

They had big hearts, though. They would have Bible studies, inviting the homeless and prostitutes into their homes. Sophie and Aiden would feed them, give them some warm clothes, and tell them about Jesus. I didn't mind it, and it didn't scare me because everyone they brought into their home had brokenness in their eyes. I felt a connection with them.

They were also very legalistic; I fell like I couldn't do anything because Jesus wouldn't approve. They wanted me to become a missionary and go to Bible school. I guess this strictness was difficult for me largely because they were telling me I needed to follow a God I didn't believe in anymore.

I hated Jesus, I hated God, I hated to hear "Let's pray about this," and I started to resent them for following God and trying to force me to follow their God. But I still went to church.

† † †

Because of what had happened between me and Carter, I left the apostolic church and started attending a new one. A pastor by the name of Luke had left the apostolic church to start his own church, and he "recruited" some of us who felt burned by Iglesia. I guess even to this day, I feel like he preyed on the weak and the ones that were hurting. Looking back now, he reminds me a lot of Pastor Henry.

Luke started a church in Brea, California, meeting in a movie theater. I dove in, helping jump-start the children's ministry, though I didn't know why I was teaching about a God I secretly hated.

Luke and I started to become friends, and he would ask me to go hang out with him. While it seemed innocent at first, eventually it turned into me going on drives with him and being coerced into giving him blow jobs behind some abandoned building. He was so manipulative, justifying his actions by explaining that he was the pastor and that this was what God wanted. So he became just another evil Christian in my mind, like my father, like Pastor Henry.

So why did I help with this church? Looking back, I think it let me put on a facade for Sophie and Aiden that proclaimed, "Hey, look, I'm going to church! I believe!"—even though at this time, I didn't believe or care. All I wanted was a voice, and I could not have one. Instead, I had all these strong personalities around me telling me what I should and shouldn't do.

Even though I was involved in church, Sophie told me once again she wanted me to go to a school called Calvary Bible School and become a missionary.

"That's not what I want for my life!" I said.

It turned into an argument between me, Sophie, and Aiden, and Aiden got so mad at me that he raised his hand as if he were going to hit me. I was shocked and sickened at this—Aiden was ordinarily such a quiet and calm man that I couldn't process the thought of physical abuse from him.

"I can't believe this," I said. "This is so repulsive."

"Get out!" Sophie said.

And that was it. I needed a new place to live and I needed a new job. Immediately.

Dolores and I were still in contact, so she invited me to stay with her for a while until I found another place and job. I packed up my belongings and moved back down to Orange County.

✝ ✝ ✝

After a few months, I managed to get on my feet. I found a job as a receptionist for a property management company and started doing really well, even saving money so I could move out on my own. I was almost to the point of having enough saved, and I dreamed of finally having my own apartment. A place to call home. Something that would be mine and no one else's, and if I had to move it would be because of me and not because someone kicked me out.

When Carter broke my nose, Pastor Declan told me to put his son in jail.

"He cannot get away with breaking your nose," he said. "I do not approve of Carter being abusive."

I didn't press charges, but I did stay in touch with Carter's father while I lived with Dolores. He told me I was like his daughter and he wanted to make sure I was doing okay.

During the months I lived with Dolores, I was in a really bad car accident. I was knocked unconscious and rushed to the emergency room. The collision wasn't my fault, so insurance took care of my medical and attorney fees, and when all was said and done I cleared about eight thousand dollars, which was enough to get me out of Dolores's house and on my own. I was so happy!

And then Pastor Declan called me and took me out to dinner with Dolores. It wasn't long before the subject of my settlement came up.

"Madyson," he said, "what you are going to do with all that money?"

"I'm going to look for a place to live," I said.

"Mija, I don't think that's a good idea."

I was kind of puzzled. "Why not?"

"It's very dangerous for a pretty girl to live on her own," he said. "I will worry about you if you're out there living on your own; I'll worry something bad might happen to you. Instead of moving out right now, you need a better car."

"I don't think I want to spend that much money on a car."

"Well you need a more reliable car than the one you have now. Why don't you buy mine? I'll sell it to you for eight thousand dollars."

I was apprehensive, because I didn't want to spend that much money on a car, but because I trusted him, I made the deal and kept living with Dolores.

I found out much later that car was probably worth only four thousand dollars.

Nevertheless, I eventually saved enough to get out of Dolores's house and move out on my own, and once that happened, my life began to turn around dramatically.

† † †

Making Jesus Happy

My Father's Daughter

2

A Broken Heart

The building that housed the property management company where I worked was a high-rise in Newport Beach, so when I received an anonymous letter that read "Take care of you" and included a check for a thousand dollars, I rented a little studio apartment nearby. I didn't care that it was small—it was mine! All mine.

There was a salon called Sun's Hair Care located in the same office building, and I became friends with the couple who owned it. They would come into our office to pay their bills, and since I was the first one they saw, we would talk. After a few months of this, they invited me to come hang out in their salon.

They were such a beautiful couple. Their names were Luis and Polly, and they not only owned the salon, but Luis had also created an entire hair care line. They traveled all over the world to do hair trade shows and sell their products.

Talking to them and being around them seemed glamorous; I would notice the fashion magazines in the salon and think, That's what I want to be. I want to be a model.

Luis was a short, Costa Rican man with thinning curly hair, but Polly was tall with green eyes and curly blonde hair, and she was always nicely dressed and put together. As I grew closer with them, people would tell me I looked like Polly; in fact, she would occasionally introduce me as her daughter and people would say they saw the resemblance. It cracked me up every time someone would say so, but I didn't mind because Polly was beautiful.

Luis and Polly asked me if I wanted to start doing hair modeling for them, and since I'd had the property management gig for a while, I was able to take vacation time and travel with them. The first time Luis asked me to do anything was a makeover photoshoot. I was so excited. At this point, I still looked like an apostolic girl: I always wore skirts, I did not wear make-up, and my hair was long, all the way down to my waist. But when Luis asked me to do a makeover, he said it consisted of cutting my hair off.

I had mixed feelings. The apostolic church had taught me that my hair was sacred and a covering, so to cut it off was tragic to me—but it also brought a sense of freedom. No one could make me keep my hair. I could make that choice. And who was God, anyway?

"Let's do this."

I went into the salon on a Saturday afternoon and Luis cut it off (I donated that hair to Locks of Love). Luis cut my hair above my shoulders, so it felt really short, but I loved it. He styled my hair, I had my makeup done by his daughter-in-law Kaitlin, and Polly dressed me in pants and a shirt that showed my midriff. That part was uncomfortable, because I was so used to wearing dresses every day and not showing any skin.

Then it was time to take the pictures. The photographer was Luis's son Adrian. He was handsome, with spiky black hair, a freakishly perfect smile, and this presence about him; when he walked into a room, you definitely noticed him. He kept coming up to me and talking to me, but I was so nervous that this handsome man was talking to me that I kind of ignored him. Plus, I was embarrassed that a guy I thought was so cute was seeing me with half my clothes on.

I don't think being ignored was something Adrian was used to. It seemed as he was used to getting a lot of attention, so when I ignored him he wasn't too happy.

When the photo shoot was over, my sister Charlotte came to take me out to lunch. She's four years older than I am, but people always thought we were twins, and when Adrian saw her, he of course immediately went up to her and starting talking with her and asked her out.

Charlotte said yes.

They went on about three dates and never saw each other again. She said he was too clingy.

Charlotte found a job in my building, working for a law firm so she could become a lawyer, and I continued to do photo shoots with Luis and Polly until Luis asked me one day if I wanted to go to a trade show in Long Beach with him, his wife, and some other models. It was one of the biggest trade shows in the hair industry, and I didn't have to think twice. I said yes immediately. It was the start of something new, something exciting.

It was a long, three-day weekend; all the models got up at three in the morning to have their hair and make-up done by seven. We would stand on stage for about twelve hours with hair that looked like a cowboy hat or some other crazy design, and people would come up touch our hair while Luis, Polly, Adrian, and their other son Brody sold their product to hair salons.

That first night, all the models, Luis, Polly, and their two sons went out to dinner. Adrian sat next to me at dinner and we talked and talked. There was suddenly something about Adrian that made him easy to be with. He was so easy to talk to; when I was around him it was like no one else was there and nothing else was going on around us. After that show we became best friends and hung out all the time. It was great.

† † †

Things in my life were good and happy, with no drama or craziness. I started to travel all over with Adrian, his family, and their company. We went to South Korea, Australia, Canada, and all over the United States; I was seeing the world and it was amazing. I went from a little girl escaping her nightly abuse by getting lost in her glow-in-the-dark stars and dreaming about the world to an independent woman traveling the world and doing things most people had never dreamed of.

Luis was asked to do a photo shoot for Modern, the number-one magazine in the hair industry. For a hairdresser, it's one of the biggest accomplishments you can have, and Luis asked if I would be his model for that shoot. Of course I said yes. Adrian was at the shoot to hang out and make sure everything ran smoothly, and we goofed off and laughed during the whole shoot. It was an amazing day.

I had started to feel so comfortable in my own skin that standing in front of the camera seemed normal; I felt free in front of it. I would start off as a blank slate, then get my hair done, my makeup done, and the finished product was art. It was something beautiful, and that beautiful thing was me. I usually felt like I couldn't wash away the secrets of my childhood, but when I would do these trade shows and photo shoots, I stepped out of my world for just a little bit and I wasn't that broken little girl—I was a beautiful creation. The day of the Modern magazine photo shoot something changed in me, and I no longer felt dirty, angry, or bitter. I simply felt beautiful.

That night, Adrian and I went out to a place close to his house for dinner, laughing and dining and having fun. Adrian then suggested we rent a movie and hang out some more, so we went to the video store and settled on watching a romantic comedy. That was one thing I loved about Adrian: he was a hopeless romantic who would watch sappy movies and liked listening to sappy love songs with me.

When we got back into his car he stopped and looked at me. "You are so beautiful," he said.

I laughed, but when he then leaned over to kiss me, I pushed him away.

"No!" I said, "You went out with my sister, and who knows what you did with her. I'm not going to be anyone's second best."

"I never did anything with Charlotte," he said. "I promise. I've wanted to be with you from day one."

I knew at the time it was just a line, so I laughed it off and ignored him, but with all the time I spent traveling with him and his family, plus the time we spent hanging out together alone, we ended up falling in love. He chased me and chased me, and eventually I gave in.

Adrian was my life. I let him in little by little, and when he first kissed me, it was like the world had stopped on perfect. He eventually asked me to marry him, which was a dream. It was the start of my fairy tale life with my best friend.

† † †

We got married and I became even closer with Luis and Polly. Luis was an odd one: a straight hairdresser who sometimes acted gay. He somehow seemed to know my story, what had happened to me as a little girl, even though I never opened up and told him. He just said to me one day, "I know," and I started to cry.

Luis told me all the time he was praying for me, and my heart started to soften to the idea of God. I didn't dare tell anyone that, though. Luis also told me even before Adrian proposed to me that he was my dad. He told me to call him and Polly Mom and Dad, and though I didn't at first, eventually I did.

I became so close with this family. I traveled everywhere with them, Adrian's brother Brody became one of my best friends, too—we worked out together every morning—while Brody's wife and I were like sisters and I loved their daughter. For the first time I was part of a real family.

Before Adrian and I were married, I lived with Luis and Polly. I would get up in the morning to go work out, then come home around seven a.m. to start the day. When I got home, Luis would always be sitting on the couch drinking his coffee.

"Come sit next to me," he would say.

"No," I always said.

"Come on."

Then I would, and then he would put his arm around me and hug me. I would pull away, but he would only hug me tighter.

"I love you and you're my daughter," he would say. "This is what a daddy does—hug you and love you. I will never hurt you, because daddies are not supposed to hurt their daughters, and one day you'll let me hug you and love you without pulling away."

I remember the day that happened. It was the day I broke their hearts.

† † †

After Adrian and I got married, I still traveled, eventually becoming the face of Sun's Hair Care. I was on every brochure and at the trade show, mine was the face on the booths. I quit my job at the property management company and started going on casting calls to model full-time. So in between doing hair shows and traveling, I was in Los Angeles trying to make a name for myself, looking up modeling websites and posting my pictures to try to get work.

Then I got an email from an LA-based producer named Benjamin who said he was producing a movie and I would be a great fit for it. I emailed Benjamin back and told him I'd never acted before, that all I'd done was model. He said that was okay—

he thought I was the right look for the part and wanted to know if I would come "read for it." I agreed.

I didn't really know what "reading for a part" was—I figured it was an audition of some sort—but if I'd known that driving to Benjamin's huge house on Mulholland Drive in the Hollywood Hills would change the course of my life so drastically, I would have never done it.

I pulled up to his house and was met by Benjamin and his production partners Charlie and Ryan. Benjamin was very tall and bald with light eyes—he looked like a construction worker to me—while Ryan was short and bald, with a little pot belly and a British accent. Charlie was an average-height Asian man. They escorted me through Benjamin's huge mansion to his office, and we sat down, they on one side of the office and me on a couch on the other side.

They handed me a script, gave me a minute to look at it, and then Benjamin said, "When you're ready, read the script like you are that person."

I was horrible.

I stumbled over my words, shaking a little, and then I just started to laugh because I knew I sucked.

When I was finished, Benjamin looked at me and said, "You do suck at acting." And we all just laughed and laughed.

Benjamin and I became good friends after that. He knew I wanted to be in the modeling business, and when I would go up to LA, I would drive up early to miss traffic and hang out at Benjamin's house with him and his assistant. It turned out Benjamin was actually a very successful producer who had funded some major movies; when I met him, however, he was in the process of inviting pretty girls to his house to "do a reading" in order to find a girlfriend who could be his wife. Since I was already married, that wasn't going to happen, but we became great friends.

† † †

Sun's Hair Care started to get busy, so Adrian started traveling a lot, sometimes without me. Our first year together was great, and mostly normal. My earliest experience of marriage was my parents yelling and fighting and saying hurtful things to each other, but Adrian and I didn't do that—we were friends who talked all the time. This is what I thought a normal marriage was supposed to be.

After that first year, things started to get kind of weird. He wanted to have sex three, four, five times a day, and he wanted to try new things that made me uncomfortable. But he was my husband, so I thought I needed to make him happy. Sometimes he would get rough, and though it bothered me, I didn't say anything because I loved him and wanted to make him happy.

One day I was so sick that I could not stop throwing up, so I took a pregnancy test. It came back positive. I was so happy that I could hardly wait to tell Adrian.

He came home and I pounced. "I have something really important to tell you," I said.

"Let's have sex first," he said

So I did. Adrian was only the second person I had been with sexually, so I didn't know that having sex that often was not normal. We did what he wanted, and then I told him.

"I'm pregnant."

Adrian looked at me. "That's okay," he said, "we'll take care of it."

"What do you mean, 'take care of it?'"

"I mean we'll take care of it."

"I want to keep it," I said.

"No," he said, "this is not the time to have kids."

"Why?"

"It just isn't."

I was devastated. I loved this man and wanted this baby. But because I loved and trusted Adrian, I trusted that he knew best. I wish now that I had questioned him more, but I didn't.

A week later he made an appointment, took me to Planned Parenthood, dropped me off, and told me to call him when it was done.

"You aren't going to stay?" I said.

"No, you need to do this alone."

This was the first time in our marriage I'd felt so alone. When I was sitting there preparing myself for my abortion, I could not stop crying, so a counselor came out and spoke with me.

"Do you want to do this?" she asked.

I nodded.

"Is anyone forcing you to do this?"

I shook my head no. Then went in the room and had an abortion.

To this day, thinking about that moment and the choice I made haunts me. I took a life God gave me. I think about how old my son or daughter would be now, and though I know Jesus has forgiven me, I find it difficult to forgive myself for taking that life. My child's life.

† † †

A few days later, Luis and Polly invited me to go to South Korea with them as a model, and I agreed. I wanted to get away from Adrian and out of California to get my mind off of what I had done.

Since international flights offered free alcohol, I drank and drank. Luis asked if I was okay and I lied to him and said yes.

We were there for a month, and it was amazing. When you are a blonde white girl in South Korea, you get treated like a celebrity just because you look so different. It was a wonderful experience, but I felt unwell the whole time. I was constantly tired, but I assumed that was because of the trade shows, the photo shoots, and time difference.

When it was time to head back, Polly looked at me with concern.

"You don't look very well," she said.

"Probably because I'm tired," I said.

"No, your throat has a huge bulge coming out of it."

I hadn't noticed it.

"When we get back you should go to the doctor and get that checked," Polly said.

We flew home, and a few days later I made an appointment with my doctor and told him about my throat and how I was feeling. He wanted to run some tests, so he swabbed my throat and took a biopsy from my cervix. About a week later, the doctor called me to come into his office and go over the results. I didn't know then that when a doctor calls you to come into their office, it is not good news.

"I would like to do an ultrasound on your thyroid," he said, "because there's a possibility you could have thyroid cancer."

I was shocked. "Cancer?" I said. "I'm so young. How can I have cancer?"

And then he doubled my shock. "You also have cervical cancer."

My life flashed before my eyes. God's punishing me because I took a life he was trying to give me, I thought.

"The good news," the doctor said, "is that with cervical cancer we could probably go in and cut it all out."

I went home and told Adrian what the doctor said. He was drinking coffee and he just looked at me with this blank look that had no emotion. He didn't say anything except that he was going to bed. I'd just told my husband I was sick—possibly very sick—and he got up and walked away.

Adrian started to look at me often with these blank stares. The world used to stand wonderfully still when I was with him, but now now it suddenly seemed really big and scary. I don't know what changed in Adrian; I did everything I could to make him happy and be the perfect partner to him, but something changed in him—and not for the better.

† † †

I went through a month of intense tests and the results were confirmed: cervical and thyroid cancer. My doctor told me he wanted to go in and surgically remove the cancer from my cervix; once I was healed from that, I could start chemotherapy and radiation for my thyroid.

The day I went in for surgery, I asked Adrian to drive me.

"No," he said.

"Aren't you going?"

"No."

My heart broke. This man I loved, my husband, was not going to be there. But Luis and Polly were. I got out of surgery at five in the evening; by midnight I was in horrendous pain. I looked at Polly, and for the first time I called her "Mom."

"Mom, I know you have Tylenol or something. Please give it to me."

Polly was one of the most patient, soft-spoken women I've ever met, but she grabbed a nurse and very sternly said, "My daughter is in pain. She needs some medicine!"

I was in such pain because the morphine drip prescription I was supposed to have had gotten mixed up during shift change at the hospital. While I waited for them to fix it, I looked at Luis longingly. "Daddy," I said, "please make the pain go away."

Luis laid his hands on my head to pray for me and I immediately fell asleep.

A few weeks later, I went to have an ultrasound on my throat, and the doctor was surprised.

"The cancer looks like it's gone," he said. "Let's run some more tests."

They did, and the tests verified that the cancer was indeed gone. I went to Luis and Polly's house that day and told them the news.

"Do you remember when you had your surgery?" Luis asked.

"Yes, I said.

"When I prayed for you and you fell asleep," he said, "I laid my hand on your throat and said, 'Jesus, please heal my daughter.' Then I felt a heat in between my hand and your throat, and at that moment I knew a miracle had happened and that Jesus had healed you."

Jesus did heal me from thyroid cancer that day, and I started to believe just a little more each day that God was real.

† † †

After I recovered my health, I started doing trade shows again. Adrian and I were having a rough time since my surgery, but I still loved him. I couldn't understand how he wasn't there for me, his wife, and I was heartbroken over it, but I went on as though nothing had happened.

It was time to travel again, so Adrian, Brody, Luis, Polly, and I all flew to Chicago for a huge trade show. After the first day, I was in our hotel room waiting for Adrian so we could take all the models and everyone who worked the show out to dinner. But when Adrian came up to the room, he had a woman with him. She was tall, brunette, and very beautiful. I'd seen her around Adrian before, but I'd always assumed she did some kind of business with him.

"May I use the restroom?" she asked.

"Of course," I said.

A few minutes later, she walked out of the restroom completely naked.

Adrian looked at me. "I want to have a threesome with you two right now," he said.

I was furious. "Adrian, you have two choices here," I said. "One: you leave with me right now and we work this out. Two: you stay and I'm on the next flight home."

I got up to leave and opened the door; when I looked back, Adrian wasn't coming.

I stood tall and left the room, making sure I was far away from the room before allowing my tears to fall. I loved this man so much it hurt. Yet my husband, my love, my best friend just rejected me and chose another woman over me.

I got in the elevator, went down one story, walked to the ice machine, fell to the floor, and started sobbing. A woman walked by and asked if I was okay; I nodded and pulled myself together enough to get back in the elevator and head to the nearest bar to drink the night away.

I was on the first flight home the next morning, and within that five-hour flight home, Adrian closed out every credit card and all our bank accounts. He came back not long after me and when he walked into the house, I was sitting on the couch having coffee just thinking, What is going on.

"Get out of my house," he said.

"I'm your wife," I said.

"This is my house. Get out."

"I'm not leaving. I love you. I gave up my life for you!"

"Get out," he said. "I don't love you anymore."

I was devastated beyond belief. I know I truly was in love with this man, and I still loved him even after he'd decided to kick me out. He was my best friend.

But no more.

I was devastated, but I left with nowhere to go. I went to Luis and Polly, but they said, "We're not going to get in the middle of your fight; you kids need to work this out. When you're married, you work it out." While I knew that was true, I didn't know what we needed to work out, because I didn't know what was broken.

Adrian shut me out of his life and wouldn't talk to me. We both were broken when we got married—I hated my parents, and my escape from my parents and previous horrible life was my husband, which wasn't healthy for Adrian, for myself, or for our marriage. Adrian's escape was me. We both tried to escape into this fairytale romance, and when the novelty wore off for him, it broke our marriage.

The problem was, I still very much loved Adrian so deeply that my heart was shattered when he said he didn't love me anymore. I felt like Adrian made my heart whole; my father had broken it and Adrian had put the pieces together.

When my husband kicked me out, I did not know what to do, so I called Benjamin.

"Come up here!" he said. "I have this huge house. You're welcome here."

Driving up to LA that day changed my life; it was the day I gave my life over to the dark side, the day my life began a huge downward spiral.

† † †

My Fathers Daughter

3

Taken For Granted

Benjamin's mansion was on a hill, with a view that overlooked Hollywood and LA. He had a huge pool, three guest houses (which he rented out), and two awesome-looking ridgeback dogs. I pulled into his driveway that day confused, hurt, angry, and disoriented.

I parked next to a blue Lexus and this woman, the girlfriend of one of the guest house renters, came out to meet me. She was a tall, beautiful brunette with light eyes.

"Are you Madyson?" she said.

"Yes."

"I heard what happened with your husband, and I'm so sorry," she said. And then, out of nowhere, she said, "You're beautiful—you should do porn."

I laughed. "Yeah, right."

"You want to go to a party with me tonight? Just have a good night?"

What did I have to lose? I just wanted to drink and not think about anything.

"Yes."

She turned to leave, telling me she'd be back to get me later that night. I don't know why I was so quick to want to hang out with a stranger, but I figured if she was at Benjamin's house, then how bad could she be?

That night we went all over Los Angles and Hollywood, and no matter where we went, we didn't wait in line. We had VIP service. This woman had stacks of hundred-dollar bills, and she spread them around. I wondered how she had so much money, and at the end of the night I asked her outright.

"What do you do?" I said.

"Porn."

She hadn't been kidding in the driveway.

"You should do it," she continued. "You're beautiful. You would make a lot of money."

"Really?"

"Yeah. You know where Benjamin's house is—just drive downhill on Mulholland you'll see a place called "Video" Entertainment. Walk in there and tell them you want to do porn." She glanced over my body. "They'll hire you."

I can't do porn; this girl is crazy, I thought. It didn't bother me that she did porn, but I sure as heck wasn't going to do it.

I went back to Benjamin's house. As I lay in a huge bed with white sheets, in an equally huge, clean white guest room with large windows, I kept thinking, What am I going to do? I have nowhere to live, no money, no job, and I am about to go through a divorce.

Maybe, just maybe, I should do a couple of videos, make some quick money and get on my feet.

I thought about doing porn all night. Our thoughts can be dangerous, especially when we're in a really bad place. That's when the devil will get in and plant thoughts to justify things we would never normally do, justify them for that moment in time. I really didn't know what porn was—I had never even seen a pornographic image or video. I knew people had sex for money, and it would have never been something I would have considered, ordinarily. But because my mind was weak and I was in such a low place, the devil pounced and put thoughts in my head.

So what did I do? I got up the next morning and drove down Mulholland Drive and into the parking lot of an In-N-Out Burger. Across the street was a huge building with a sign on top that read "Video" Entertainment.

I sat in that parking lot for what seemed like a lifetime and battled with my thoughts. Should I do this? Should I not?

I finally talked myself into driving across the street and pulling into the parking lot, saying to myself, It's not going to hurt if I go inside and just ask how to get into porn. So I got out of my silver Volkswagen beetle convertible and walked through the glass doors and up some stairs to a huge reception desk with a gorgeous blonde woman.

I walked straight up to her. "What do I need to do if I want to do a couple of porn videos?"

"Hold on," she said. She got up walked to an office in the back, and returned with a man who was apparently a producer. When he walked out, he was kind of sleazy and greasy-looking; I was afraid, but stood strong like I knew what I was doing. I don't know why I was afraid—he just seemed to me like a bad man, and he gave me the creeps.

The producer walked over to me, looked me up and down, and said, "I will pay you to sleep with me right now."

I just stared back at him with a disgusted look.

"No?" he said. "Okay, fine." He handed me a business card. "Here's a number for Models of Los Angeles. Ask for Sebastian—he's the number-one porn agent in the business."

I took the card, thanked him, and turned to walk out.

"You'll make a lot of money, kid," the producer said. "You have an innocence about you. Guys love that. They love their girls to look young, and you look young. Sebastian is going to make a lot of money off you."

When I walked out, I didn't think, I just did. It's hard to explain, but it was like the person I really am left my body temporarily and whoever was left in my body was just going to do whatever it took to survive.

I called the number on the card and asked for Sebastian.

"He isn't in," the voice on the other end of the line said. "What is this about?"

"I want to do porn."

"Can you come in and meet with us right now?"

"Yes."

† † †

I drove across town to Models of Los Angeles, which was located in a high-rise building above a bank. I walked into their third-floor office and saw about three or four people at the front desk.

"I'm here to see Sebastian," I said, and one of them handed me a form.

"Go sit on the couch over there and fill this form out," the receptionist said.

This form was like nothing I'd ever seen before. It had a section at the top with check boxes for what I would and would not do, with options like BJ, DP, GG, BG.

I was confused, so I asked a girl setting next to me, "What does this mean?"

She looked at me with this weird expression. "Have you ever had sex before?"

"Yes, of course."

"BJ is blow job, DP is double penetration, GG is girl-girl, and I'm sure you get the picture."

I thought at that second, Get up and walk out.

But then I heard someone call my name. "Madyson?"

I turned and saw a skinny guy with blonde hair that was kind of greasy. "Hi," he said, "my name is Evan and I am one of the agents and owners here. Sebastian isn't here yet but will be in a few minutes."

We went to an office where Evan asked me questions about why I wanted to do porn and in my innocence, I told him my sob story about making a few videos to get some money, get on my feet, and then be done.

While we were talking this really buff, somewhat handsome guy walked in. This was Sebastian.

"Are you Madyson?"

"Yes," I said.

"Get naked."

"What?"

"Get naked," he said. "I need to make sure your body looks okay for the videos."

So I did it. I took off my clothes in front of Sebastian and Evan, thinking about the first time my father told me to take off my clothes, like it was natural for men to tell me get naked. My father, my husband, and now these two strangers.

"You are beautiful," Sebastian said. "No tattoos? You'll make us a lot of money."

After I got dressed, Sebastian handed me a contract. "Once you sign this," he said, "it means you're agreeing to be my girl for the next year."

I signed the contract not knowing that, at that moment, I signed my life over to Sebastian.

"You need to go get a tan," Evan said. "You're too white."

"I don't have money for anything," he said.

"Okay, let's go."

"Right now?"

"Yeah," he said. "We gotta get you booked."

† † †

After the tanning salon, Evan took me to Aim Healthcare, a mandatory testing facility where actors in the adult film industry all go every twenty-seven days to get tested for HIV, gonorrhea, and chlamydia. When you go to a video shoot, you must bring that test with you before you can actually shoot the video, and the dates need to be current.

I stayed at Benjamin's house for the time being, and was still really close with Luis and Polly, going to hair trade shows with them and still modeling. I did not dare tell them what I was about to do, though.

Evan called me as soon as Aim gave me a clean bill of health. "We have a lot of shoots booked for you," he said. "But you can't go by your real name—you need a stage name."

Adrian and I had talked a lot previously about changing my name, since I did not want the name my mother or father gave me, so I had already started the process of legally changing my name to the one Adrian wanted me to have: Bri.

And that's the name I used for porn.

Evan said it was perfect.

† † †

The first shoot they had booked for me was with another girl. I didn't know until I showed up for the shoot, and so I took the producer aside and said, "I don't want to do this. I'm not gay. I don't want to be with a girl."

"You're doing it," he said. "Stop whining."

One of the other women who was there handed me a pill. "Here, take this," she said. "It will calm you down."

I took it and then got ready for the shoot. While the cameras were rolling, I mentally went somewhere else and became the little girl looking at the glow-in-the-dark stars, just trying to get through an hour of hell.

†　†　†

For a few weeks I went back in forth between Orange County and LA until Luis and Polly finally said I could stay with them while I was in Orange County until I got on my feet. They asked me what I was doing in LA so much, and I lied and told them I had modeling gigs.

I was lost and did not know what to do. I had not talked to Sophie in a long time, but I needed help and I didn't know where else to go. One day I was at the Irvine Spectrum trying to recruit hair models for Luis and Polly when I ran into Peyton, Sophie's friend who had produced the Fashions of Each Era shows we had done as children. She hugged me and told me to call her. I thought that would be the last time I saw Peyton; little did I know I would end up living with her years later.

She also encouraged me to call Sophie, which I did, arranging to visit her at her house. We met soon afterward and I told her everything I was doing and that I needed help.

"You got married and didn't tell me," she said.

"Sophie, I need help. I've started doing porn videos that I don't want to do, and I'm living with Adrian's parents, but I know he isn't happy with me there. I need somewhere to live and help to get on my feet."

I'm not going to help you," Sophie said.

"You're my sister," I said. "I need help."

"Madyson, you've sinned against Jesus and against me and Aiden. You need to apologize to us for first doing porn and cutting us out of your life."

I looked at her, so broken, so torn. "But I need your help."

"No."

I hated Jesus all over again. After being with Luis and seeing him read his Bible every morning, and feeling Luis and Polly's love, I was starting to let Jesus into my heart little by little. The Jesus I grew up with and heard about definitely isn't the Jesus I know now—but that's the Jesus I knew then. The Jesus that Sophie, my father, Pastor Henry, Pastor Declan, and my mom made up; the Jesus who would justify who they were and what they were doing.

"Madyson, you need to repent. In front of me and Aiden."

Repent to her? I wanted a sister, I wanted her to just hug me and say, "We will work through this."

"Screw this," I said as I got up and left.

† † †

Adrian and I were trying to talk and stay friends in order to get through the divorce, though I think his parents had a lot to do with that. About a month into my porn career, Adrian called me and asked me to come to the offices after hours to meet with him. When I walked in, no one was there but him.

"Is there something you want to tell me?" he said.

"No."

Adrian turned his computer screen around toward me and showed me one of my own porn videos. The accountant for Sun's Hair Care had found it by Googling my porn name "Bri" and had sent the link to Adrian.

I broke down and started to cry uncontrollably. "Adrian, I hate you! I'm your wife. You abandoned me. You left me. I could have died and you weren't there."

He stood up to hug me, and I just hit him and hit him, over and over. He let me.

I eventually stopped and fell to the floor on my knees with my head in my hands. "What have I done?" I said.

Adrian got down on the floor with me and I fell into his arms and cried and cried.

He tried to make me laugh. "You used our name?"

It worked. "I didn't know what else to pick," I said, and we laughed.

Even though we were going through so much, he was safe. I loved him; he had my heart.

† † †

I was scheduled to travel to South Korea again with Luis and Polly, and Adrian encouraged me to tell them; I agreed to do so after we got back.

Going to South Korea was the last thing I wanted to do, but I did it anyway. Unfortunately, on the flight, the same accountant sent a link to my video to Adrian's brother Brody. He was angry that I had done porn, that I didn't tell him, and that I was jeopardizing the integrity of the company.

When we landed, Brody called me on Luis's international phone and laid into me.

"Madyson, you are telling my parents once you are settled into the hotel, do you understand?"

"Yes, I do. I will."

There was a pause, and then Brody said, "Why?"

"I didn't know where else to go," I said. "I went to your parents and they told me to work it out; I went to my sister and she didn't help. It was my last option."

"No, it wasn't," he said. "You could have come to me and Kaitlin."

I kept thinking of everyone I loved and how I was breaking their hearts, and I knew that the two people who loved me the most were going to shatter with this news.

We got to the hotel, and after we were settled, I went to Luis and Polly's room.

"Can we talk?"

They invited me in, and I sat down on the bed while they sat on the ledge by the window. I started to get teary-eyed. All I could say was, "I'm sorry, I'm sorry."

"What are you sorry for?" Polly asked.

"I didn't know what to do," I said. "Adrian took the money from me. I'm sorry."

"What are you sorry for, Madyson?" Luis asked.

I gathered myself. "Out of desperation, I have done videos."

They had confused looks on their faces and I knew they didn't get it.

"I've been doing porn videos to make money."

Again I fell to the floor, feeling totally broken. Luis sat down on the floor with me and held me, and I let him. For the first time, he was really my daddy—I sat in his arms without squirming and without trying to get away. Then Polly sat down next to me and they both held me for about a good hour while I cried and cried.

They cried with me.

Looking back, I wish that I had had more of those moments with them—and not just when I broke their hearts into a million pieces. Every choice this couple made in my life was because they loved me so truly, never because they wanted something from me. This was so apparent and real to me that day when, instead of yelling or getting angry, they sat on the floor and allowed me to cry and comforted me.

"We'll get through this," they said.

When we arrived home a week later, Adrian wanted to go out with me, so I met up with him at the Sun's Hair Care office.

"Madyson," he said, "I have a question and if you are completely honest with me, then we will get through this rough patch and we can fix our marriage."

"Okay, what's the question?"

"How many videos have you done?"

I honestly didn't know how many I had done at that point and couldn't answer the question completely; even to this day I couldn't answer that question. Was it hundreds? I just don't know.

I lied and told him two.

"That's it," he said. "You've only done two videos."

"Yup."

"I don't care how many you have done," he said, "but if you're not honest with me, we will never be together."

I promised up and down the wall it was only two. Why? Why did I lie? Because I felt like the real number would break his heart, and I couldn't do that anymore. I could not break his family's heart anymore. I was so young. He had shattered my heart and I, for some reason, was still concerned about shattering his. Plus, I think deep down there was a part of me that didn't trust his promise to stay with me if I told him the truth.

Sebastian also called me when I got back and told me they had lined up a shoot for me in a few days. I didn't want to go, but I was afraid. Sebastian was scary; he was someone that you just didn't say "no" to, and I'd signed that contract, so I just agreed to do the shoot.

† † †

Throughout this entire process of going through a divorce while doing these adult films, I felt the need to find a church to attend. I don't know what my thought was in going to church—maybe somewhere deep down inside, I thought the church could help me. Maybe a little part of me believed that there was a different kind of Jesus—a loving one, not the Jesus everyone in my life seemed to tell me about. I saw that loving Jesus in Luis and Polly, and I had this void I thought church could fill.

I never would have imagined that multiple churches were involved in the adult film industry. Growing up in Orange County you hear about the hip new things, including the hip new churches, and one was called Radiant Church, with multiple services and two locations. They actually had services in a night club as well as in a church building. I kept hearing about it, so I started going.

After my first couple weeks there, I met a girl whose name was Nora. She was sweet, and not what I was used to being around. She was a church girl—she didn't know much about the outside world; she knew the church and that was it. She didn't drink or party; her dream was to find a husband and have a family and a white picket fence. She had long brown hair, never wore makeup, and was kind of frumpy-looking, but was very sweet and tried hard to become my friend, inviting me to coffee and Bible studies.

I kept her at a distance because she wasn't like me and she had never done anything bad like porn. Most of the time I would stand her up and cancel at the last minute. I think people somehow saw porn on me—not porn or sex specifically but rather a desperation for something more, for a need to be rescued.

Nora invited me to go to a "life group," which is basically a group of people getting together and talking about a topic within the Bible or about the service from the previous Sunday. I relented and went. It was okay, and I thought, I'll keep going. I mean, I'm doing adult films, so going to a Bible study couldn't really hurt me, right?

I went there for a few weeks and the life group leader by the name of Nathan took me aside one night and asked me to go on a date with him. I told him thanks, but I was married. Even though I was going through a divorce, Adrian and I were trying to work on things and I was in absolutely no position in my life to go on a date.

† † †

The morning came for the shoot Sebastian had booked me for, and when I got there, I was in a trance. The entire drive up to LA, all I could think about was Adrian and his family and how much I'd broken their hearts.

After my makeup was done, the producer said, "Madyson, it's time to shoot. Get naked."

Those words triggered something in me and I freaked out.

"No!" I screamed. "I can't do this! I'm done! I don't want to do this!"

The producer said firmly, "You are doing this."

"No!" I screamed again.

The producer quickly got Sebastian on the phone. "You're doing this video," he said calmly.

"No, I can't do this anymore," I said.

"You signed a contract with me. I own you and your body."

I started to cry. "Sebastian, I can't do this anymore. I have hurt my family enough."

"You mean Adrian, Luis, Polly, Brody..." He named all off my sisters, my parents, and every single person who was involved in my life. He named names, home addresses, work addresses, what they did for a living, their kids' names. Everything. Then he said, "You hurt your family by doing porn? They'll be really hurt if you don't do this video. Go back and do this video or your family is dead and then you are dead."

I was apprehensive, but what else could I do? I put down the phone and started to get ready. The producer was annoyed, the male "talent" that was in the video with me was annoyed, and since I was crying, I asked them to give me a minute to calm down.

"No," the producer said, "we'll go with it and film this as a rape scene."

He called action and the male talent grabbed me, slapped me, tore my clothes off, and threw me on the ground. He started calling me a slut and whore, saying things like "sluts like to get raped" and "sluts like it rough."

I was raped on film.

It was so terrifying. The whole time, all I could think about was Adrian, his family, and all the kids involved. I was starting to understand I was in a world I would not be able to get out of.

When it was all said and done, I got dressed and tried to leave, but the producer stopped me.

"You can't leave. You need to go see Sebastian."

"Okay, I'll drive over there right now."

"No," he said, "you'll go with Sebastian's driver."

I didn't know why, but I didn't have a choice in the matter. One of Sebastian's drivers was there, and he told me to get in his car and go with him.

When we arrived at the agency, Sebastian was very angry. He took me into an office with no windows and threw me up against the wall.

"If you ever pull that shit again, I will kill everyone you care about, make you watch, and then kill you," he said. "Don't cross me. You are making me so much money right now." He calmed down a bit and then said, "Do I need to move you into my house or can I trust you to show up to every shoot I book for you?"

I was shaking. "I promise, I promise I will be at every booking."

And that was that.

Sebastian's driver drove me back to retrieve my car. I cried the entire drive back to Orange County.

† † †

I had life group that night and I wondered whether someone there could help me. Was it safe? I thought. Should I say something? I'll just go and see if an opportunity arises to get help. It seemed like when anything traumatic happened to me in the past, I went on with the day like nothing had happened, burying what was going on deep inside.

When I walked into the apartment where they held the life group, everyone was sitting there silently and staring at me. I thought it was because I was a little late, but I'd texted Nora to tell her I was going to be late, so that couldn't be it. I came in and found a seat, and Nathan said, "Madyson, we're glad you're here. We're going to watch a video tonight."

Nathan was a kind of chunky tall guy with a shaved head and very round face, and I thought when I walked in that there was something creepy about the look in his eyes. It was this look like he was undressing me with his eyes, a look I get now from men I know have seen films of me.

It doesn't matter where I am—work, church, or playing at the park with my son—I know who knows who I used to be because of that look in their eyes.

Well, as you might have guessed, the video that went into the TV that night was one of my porn videos. I was devastated.

I got up and said very calmly, "Turn it off."

No one did anything.

I got a little louder. "Turn it off!"

Still no one did anything.

I started to scream. "Turn it off! Turn it off!"

Someone finally did.

Nora tried to touch my arm like she cared. "Please sit down," she said. "It's okay. We want to talk."

I was shaking. I looked at her and pulled my arm away real quick. I mean, come on, what was going on? That day I'd already been raped, beaten up, and threatened, and now this? Nathan looked at me with eyes that were as evil as Sebastian's.

"You need to explain to us why you are doing this," he said. "This is wrong, and if you don't explain to us why you're doing it, then you're going to hell."

What is going on? I thought. This is Sophie's house all over again. Hell itself at this point would be better than the hellish life I had lived, so I walked up to Nathan, got really close to his face, and said, "I'll explain why I'm doing porn as soon as you explain why you're watching it."

I walked out.

A guy in the group named Paul followed me out. "Madyson, wait!" he said. "Are you okay? I didn't know they were going to do that."

Nora was right behind him. "I'm sorry," she said. "We should not have done that."

I didn't acknowledge Nora, but I did say to Paul, "If you did not know, then you should have stood up as soon as they started it and said it was wrong. That makes you just as guilty."

They both tried to stop me, but I didn't want anything to do with them or anyone else at this point. Adrian and I were trying to work on our relationship, so I went back to his house, but it was kind of late at this point. He was asleep, so I didn't get in the bed with him; I laid on the couch instead and cried and cried.

I did not know what to do. I should have told Adrian what was going on, but I was scared because I'd lied to him and promised I wouldn't do another video. He would blame me, he would hate me—and to be honest, I secretly hated him because I blamed him for putting me in a desperate situation.

As I considered it, though, I realized I couldn't handle the rejection of the man I was so in love with again, not after everything. This time in my life felt as though I was trying to hold all the pieces together, and yet everything was falling apart around me. I had become that broken cross I shattered in Pastor Henry's office as a teenager, and at this point there was no gluing me back together.

I should have gone to Luis and Polly; they could have helped me. I could have gone to Brody and his wife Kaitlin, but Sebastian's threat stayed in my head.

I just cried myself to sleep.

† † †

Eventually, Adrian found out I was still doing porn. He wanted absolutely nothing to do with me, and neither did Brody or Kaitlin. All they had to do was Google my porn name and they could see very easily that I was still doing porn—and more than a couple of films.

Luis and Polly sat me down and said, "You are our daughter, but Adrian is our son and we stand with him on this. We need to part ways. You're the face of Sun's Hair Care and what you are doing could jeopardize our livelihood."

At that moment I stopped caring about what happened to me. It's for the best they are not in my life because now they won't be harmed or hurt by me anymore, I thought.

"I love you," Luis said.

"I love you," Polly said.

That was the moment I gave up. I had no fight left.

✝ ✝ ✝

Before I continue with my story, I want to say this: Luis and Polly became my mom and dad. The parents who gave me life are donors in my mind; donors who created a life but did not want to be responsible for it.

Luis and Polly took responsibility. They forgave me when they first found out I was doing porn. They held me like a mommy and daddy that day in Korea.

When I think about Jesus and how he forgives us when we mess up, how he holds us and carries us through our struggles, the image I carry is the compassion, love, and forgiveness my mom and dad (Luis and Polly) gave me in that moment.

If I could say anything to them, I would say I'm sorry. I'm sorry I took the life of your grandbaby, I'm sorry I could have ruined your company by doing porn, I'm sorry for not being honest and I would say… I would say, "I'm sorry; please forgive me."

Then I would say… thank you. Thank you for showing me that day who Jesus was and what Jesus—the real Jesus—is all about.

If it were not for them, I'm sure I would still hate the Jesus that was thrown in my face all the time, the Jesus people used for their gain. They gave me that little faith of a mustard seed that I carried with me for years and years; it was all I needed.

I love Luis and Polly for being a mom and dad to me, because it was something I hadn't experienced until I met them.

† † †

4

Sheep In Wolves Clothing

When Adrian and his family cut me off, I went back to live with my friend Benjamin and continued to do porn. I knew I was trapped and needed to get out somehow, so I decided to call the main pastor at Radiant Church, Pastor Matthew. He was a pastor at one of the largest churches in Orange County, so surely he would know someone who could help me. I need to trust someone sometime, I thought. Maybe I will start with him.

I don't know why I even thought of trusting anyone in this church after what had happened at the life group, but I called anyway to set up an appointment. All I said on the phone was my name and that I wanted to set an appointment with Pastor Matthew, and the receptionist said, "Hold on." A few seconds later, she got right back on the line and said, "Can you come to the church today and meet with Matthew?"

"Yes, of course," I said. "The sooner, the better. I need help."

When I got there I told this Pastor Matthew everything. I told him about Adrian and our broken marriage, Luis and Polly, porn, and Sebastian. I said I need help.

Matthew put his hand on my arm and said, "Don't worry. We'll make sure it's okay." He was a little overweight with a bald head. I had not really seen him close up before, and I remember that when I was talking to him I had an unsettling feeling. He had the eyes of those men who know who I am or what I have done. I just didn't know yet what that meant.

He did not say "I" when he said he would take care of everything, he said "we," and when his hand was on my arm, I felt this creepy feeling and moved my arm away.

"Okay, I need a bit of time," he said. "Will you stay here?"

"Okay."

"Madyson," he said, "promise me you won't leave." Then, with a stern, desperate voice, he said, "Stay here."

"Okay."

"You want anything to eat?"

"I'm okay."

He left the room and was gone for a long time. Some girl came in every fifteen minutes to check on me, and I did not realize it was to make sure I was still sitting there. I should have gotten up and run, never coming back, but I just sat there for almost two hours.

Matthew finally returned with someone and said, "Madyson, you're going to go with this guy now."

I looked at Matthew, then looked at the man who was with him, and did that about twenty disbelieving times in a row.

It was Sebastian's driver. He was there to take me to Sebastian's house.

I knew right then and there my life was over. Either he was going to kill me or I wasn't going to have any more freedom.

"You're supposed to help me, Pastor Matthew!" I said.

"You'll help me sometime," he said. "Don't worry. This is for the best."

The driver grabbed my arm really hard and said, "Get in the car and don't make a scene." So I did.

We drove up to LA to Sebastian's house. It was a huge, white house with a lot of trees and bushes that covered up the windows. It was painted a clean, bright white, but driving up to the house, you felt darkness and evil coming from it, as if what went on inside was something you never wanted to know.

Sebastian was there already and he said, "This is your home now. If you try to leave, one of my guards here will let me know and you'll be sorry."

I was devastated.

"I told you I owned you," he said.

He then had his driver to take me to his room, where there was a piece of lingerie waiting on the bed.

"Put that on," the driver said.

I was scared and didn't want to, but I did.

Then Sebastian walked in and looked me over. "I've been waiting a long time for this," he said.

Then he raped me. Over and over, for hours on end.

I could barely walk afterward.

Sebastian took me to my room, where I immediately got in the shower and just sat down. It was like everything that happened to me as a little girl was happening again as an adult; I was the little girl in the shower once more, trying to scrub off the filth of this man, with blood running down my legs.

I thought in the shower, What if I never drove down that hill? Why did I go and hang out with that girl? Why did she tell me to do porn?

I was really scared of what was going to happen now. Would someone come looking for me? In Sebastian's house, someone was always with me. If I took a shower, someone stood outside the bathroom. If I was in my room, someone stood outside the door. If Sebastian booked me for a video shoot or a nude shoot, someone took me, stayed with me until I was done, and took me back to the house.

† † †

Up until this point I only did "normal" videos. You might find that to be a strange way of thinking about it, but to me this just meant having what I thought of as normal sex and doing it on video.

For the first week living in Sebastian's house, things were normal in the sense that I continued making the same type of videos I had been doing. And then one day things changed. I thought I was already in hell at that point, but what happened next was the real hell.

Sebastian came into the room where I was staying and said, "You will not have your own room anymore; you're going to have a roommate. I'm moving her here from northern California. Be nice. You guys will be great friends."

"Okay."

"Tomorrow is not going to be your typical day. You're going to do a video shoot and then I have some people I want you to meet."

"What does that mean?"

"I just have some people that I want you to meet."

I knew enough at this point not to question him, simply to do what he said. When I was finished with my video shoot the next day, I got ready to leave but the driver said, "You're staying. You have an appointment."

In LA, porn shoots are done in multiple locations. Some are done in rented mansions, some are done in studios, and some are even done in public. It just depends on what the producer and film company are looking for.

That day we were shooting at the house of the producer himself. All the crew and everyone else had left, and now it was just the producer and me.

"You have an appointment with me," he said.

"Yeah, I guess," I said.

"Do you know what we're going to do?"

"No, I don't."

He smiled. "Great. Go up to the bedroom and put on what is laid out on the bed."

I didn't want to, but I did. It made me wonder if, when Sebastian had set up a similar scene at his home and then raped me, he was testing me to see if I would do what men said or if he would have problems with me. Life was starting to seem like déjà vu. History was repeating itself; all men wanted sex and all Christians wanted some kind of apology like they were Jesus Christ themselves.

The producer came upstairs, all slimy and creepy, and said, "Take my hand." I did, and he then led me into a bedroom with chains and whips. I freaked. I tried to run, but I could not get past him. He grabbed me and handcuffed me to these two pillars, one on each side, and began to beat me, force me to give him oral sex, and then rape me.

This went on all night, and when he was done, he removed the cuffs and said, "You can leave now." I wanted to take a shower, but I wanted to leave even more.

The driver was still there. "You have a break for a few hours," he said, "so I'll take you to the house so you can get cleaned up, and then we will be going to Orange County for a few days."

I was sore, I was bleeding from being raped, and my wrists had rings around them from the cuffs, so at that moment when the driver told me I had a few-hour break, I checked out of my body and my emotions disappeared. It was at that moment when I decided to have no emotions whatsoever. I would not cry, laugh, nothing.

They can do what they want, but they will not get a reaction out of me, not even anger.

† † †

When I went back to the house I went to my room and showered. I scrubbed my body, but I could never scrub hard enough. Any emotion I had, I expressed where no one could see me: in the shower. I cried and cried.

When I got out, there was this girl by the name of Bree in the room. This struck me as funny because I had recently changed my stage name from Bri to "Fayth," which was also funny because that was the one thing I didn't have. Bree was skinny and frail, and by looking at her I knew I was not going to make it out alive. She was beautiful but defeated.

"Hi, I'm Bree," she said.

"I'm Fayth."

No one in this industry knew each other's real names; everyone went by their stage names.

She came up to me and hugged me and started to cry. At that moment I wanted to cry with her, but I didn't because of my promise that no one would see emotion. Looking back, I wish I had let her see my tears.

"We have a trip in a few hours," she said.

"Yes."

"Do you know where we're going?"

"No," I said. "Do you?"

"You don't want to know."

Then she went to her bed and fell asleep. I wanted desperately to ask her where we were going, but I didn't. I just fell asleep with her.

† † †

A few hours later, the driver woke us up and told us to get our bags downstairs. That was odd to me since we usually didn't pack anything for shoots, but Bree and I did what he said. When we got in the car, Bree put her head against the window and looked out as her tears started to fall. When I saw that, I was scared, but I knew I needed to be strong, if not for myself then for her. It's funny how quickly strong bonds can be formed with a stranger when you go through something horrific thing together; within a few hours, over just a few words spoken aloud, you find yourselves close friends. I just knew at that moment that Bree needed me—or maybe the honest truth is that I needed her.

When I saw the tears come down from her face, I placed my hand on hers and held it all the way to Orange County.

Growing up in Orange County, I was familiar with the entire drive, so I noticed we were driving towards Radiant Church, but we did not go there; we went the club where Radiant Church held services. It was called the Show Club.

When we showed up, there were about ten other girls there, as well as a bartender asking if we wanted anything. Some girls took something, some didn't. Bree did; I didn't. Then the driver came up to me, handed me one of the drinks, and made me drink it. I started to feel loopy and not all there, which wasn't such a bad thing. I just wasn't sure what he'd given me.

After about thirty minutes, a bunch of men walked in. I don't know how many because I was so loopy, but I did recognize one: it was Pastor Matthew. I foolishly thought for a second he was finally going to help me, help Bree... but he came up to me and said to someone, "I'll take her."

I was quite disoriented at this point from whatever had been in my drink, but I could tell we were driving somewhere. This time, I wasn't sure exactly where we were going. It was a house in Orange County, and when we got there, Pastor Matthew said, "This will be your home for the next few days."

For those few days, the pastor of one of the largest churches in southern California raped, beat, sodomized, and tortured me.

He injected me with something every few hours, something that left me in and out of it for days. Finally, my time was up, and he said to me, "This is our last day together for now, but it won't be the last."

When the driver came to get me I could barely walk from everything Pastor Matthew had done to me physically and the chemicals he'd put in my body, Somehow, though, before I left, I leaned over and whispered in his ear, "Your time will come."

I don't know why I said it and to this day I don't know what it meant, because Matthew is still a pastor of a huge church in Orange County.

Every couple of weeks Bree and I would go to Orange County and different pastors, youth pastors, and leaders in the church would take a girl for a few days, act out their fantasies, and then be done.

You may wonder how I know they were leaders or pastors. I knew them because I visited many different churches while I was with Adrian and his family. I knew their faces, I knew who they were. Even now, their faces are engrained in my memory.

Some of the pastors would say what they did for a living, thinking it gave them some kind of power, and sometimes at this club I would hear them talking about what their sermon would be for that Sunday service.

Matthew picked me every couple of months, but I never spoke to him again; I just let him do his thing and was done with it.

Throughout this time, Bree and I became close. She started to look frailer and sicker to me, but she was my best friend, my family. When I was with her it was the only time I would laugh. Even though I opened up and showed her laughter, I still never showed weakness. Bree and I talked about our families, we talked about our dreams, we talked about what we would do if we could get out of porn, and we talked about trying to get help each other get out. She told me stories that horrified me of things that were done to her, but I couldn't show her fear. I needed to be strong.

Sebastian came into our room one night and told me, "You're coming with me to my other house and staying with me tonight."

"Okay." Like I said before: you don't question Sebastian.

When we got to his house, he had set up a romantic scene; I was greeted with lit candles, and when he took me to his bedroom he had champagne already on ice. He poured me some and said, "You get the privilege of being with me tonight."

I didn't want to have sex with him again, but I knew I needed to act as if I enjoyed what he was doing to me; I did not want to face the consequences of acting otherwise. So we had sex, and then he said, "You'll sleep next to me tonight, and then you're going to go on a little trip in a few months to northern California. There's another girl I'm going to have stay out at the house with you and Bree, and I want you guys to take care of her. Take care of her like you take care of Bree."

I was confused about why Sebastian acted as if he cared about one of his girls; he didn't truly care about anything but himself and money. When the night was over, though, he gave me a week off, and I was happy with that.

† † †

In that week off I slept a lot. When I was asleep, I didn't have to think, and dreaming was better than reality. Plus, dreams are one thing no one can steal from you.

When the new girl, Ann, arrived at the house, she wasn't fragile or sick-looking like Bree; she just seemed like she needed to shower. She was tall, brunette, and very pretty. She immediately took to Bree and me, but Bree wouldn't talk to her at first. I did, naively.

When Ann told us stories about what had happened to her, she would cry and shake; it seemed real. It made me scared.

The night before the three of us were supposed to go on the trip Sebastian had mentioned, Ann said "Bree and Faith, let's play a game."

"What kind of game?" Bree asked.

"Truth or dare."

Well, what could that hurt? It was just truth or dare.

Ann started off the game. Some of her questions were about our fears: What is your biggest fear? What are things you would never want done to you? What do you think the worst way to die would be? I answered her, thinking she was in the same boat as we were, so it couldn't hurt trusting her. I was wrong.

The morning we were supposed to leave, Sebastian and Evan came to the house to pick us up, and Sebastian announced, "Evan is going with you since you're all flying. Don't talk to anyone and don't try anything because I will be watching your families."

At this point, after all of my experience dealing with Sebastian, I was so scared I didn't even breathe without permission; I was certainly not going to try to get help from someone at the airport.

When we landed in northern California, there was a driver waiting to take us to our destination, and we soon pulled up to an enormous warehouse. We walked in and saw offices with people on the phone, and it looked inside like a normal business center.

"You guys are all going into makeup," Evan said, pointing.

Bree and I turned to obey, but Ann stayed. I looked at her and said, "Are you coming?"

She just got a smirk on her face and said, "Have fun."

I knew then that she had set us up, and I immediately regretted telling her my fears.

What was going to happen?

I took Bree's hand again and told her I loved her. I don't know why I said it; I just felt like I needed to tell her.

We went into makeup and were separated. I don't know where they took Bree, but they took me downstairs from the offices to a bunch of rooms. The first one I went into looked like a dungeon, with concrete floors and various chains on the ceiling, walls, and floors. In the middle of the room was a huge round tank filled with water, with different devices hooked up to it.

I got my makeup done and the makeup artist said, "Okay, get naked." Then another man came by and said, "Come with me." He threw me into the dungeon-like room, but right before he did, I felt a prick in my butt—an injection. Sebastian's people had given me drugs before, but this time I had an unusual response; I felt tingly and giggly.

I had felt these pricks before, and usually afterward I would feel sleepy and my body would feel somewhat numb. This time around was different. I felt giddy and happy, but deep down under whatever drugs they'd given me, I was terrified. The room started to spin in a good way, in a way that made me want to dance. I didn't know what drug I had received, but I liked it.

The male talent walked in and said, "Oh wow, you are so pretty." He was naked, of course, a short, older man with gray hair, and right behind him came the camera crew. "Are you ready to shoot this scene?" he asked, and I laughed, my reflexes out of my control from the drugs, and said yes. Deep down, I was angry that I was laughing and showing emotion, but I couldn't help it. The drug they gave me made me out of control.

The male took each of my arms and chained them to the wall, then he took my big toe on each foot and chained them to some balls. Then I heard the chains making noise and discovered I was being lifted up off the ground. Once I was in the air, the camera crew started to record and the male talent started to throw water on my face over and over, for what seemed like hours. I thought I was going to drown, but something in me fought against it. If I'm going to die, I sure as hell won't let these idiots kill me.

I don't know how long it took, but eventually he stopped. He took me down. I couldn't walk or even stand, but it didn't really matter; he pushed me onto the concrete floor and when I fell to the ground, he got on top of me, told me to perform oral sex, and forced himself inside my mouth really hard, to where I felt him inside my throat. When I would gag, he would hit me and throw water in my face.

"These viewers don't like gaggers! They want to know you're enjoying it!"

I wanted to scream, I'm not enjoying this! I wanted to scream, I hate you! I wanted to get up and run, run so far away, but I just lay there and let him do whatever he wanted while being filmed. I was raped and beaten for what seemed like hours.

When he was finished raping me, he ejaculated all over my face and told me to swallow it, but I closed my mouth and wouldn't do it. This made him angry, so he pulled my hair and said, "Get up."

He hooked me into the contraption that was in the middle of the room. It was this large tank of water, kind of like a place where people get baptized, with a chair on the side that had straps on the feet and straps on the hands. It looked like an electric chair from old movies. He hooked me up, then the chair pivoted back and dunked me completely into the water.

At first I fought it, shaking my head, but the more I did that, the longer he left me under. It felt like it would never end, and the film crew never left. They caught everything on camera.

When this "talent" was finally finished, he unchained me and left me in the middle of the room, naked and wet. Someone finally came to get me, and though I was disoriented, I recognized it as Ann. Then I realized I'd told her my biggest fear was drowning to death, since I liked to surf and be in the ocean.

It turned out Sebastian had planted her in the house so she could get information from Bree and me about our fears. This way, Sebastian could have a more realistic video shoot—with truly terrified talent—and make more money.

Ann said, "Let's go. I'm going to get you touched up for the next video."

When I went into the makeup room, Bree was already in there. She did not look good, appearing bruised and beaten.

"Hey," I said to her, "are you okay?"

The makeup artist said, "Don't talk to her."

I complied. I wish I had said, "Don't give up," or "You'll be okay" or anything, really, but my fear kept me quiet.

I didn't know then that, later on that day, the makeup artist would hand me a phone, and Sebastian would be on the other end telling me that Bree was dead. That's all he would say. I wouldn't ask any questions, instead just handing the phone back and holding every emotion in.

Bree really did die that day. I am sure it was from the torture she endured in that building in northern California. When we met for makeup between shoots, I saw in her eyes that she had no fight left; she just wanted to go. I loved Bree, and I wish I had tried to save her that day. I will never know if there was something I could have done, because I didn't try. Will I ever forgive myself for not saying anything to Bree? I can't answer that. All I know is she was my friend and I wasn't hers when she needed it the most.

✝ ✝ ✝

Before I go on, I need to say something about Bree's death. She and I never talked about Jesus because, well, I hated Jesus at that point in my life. But thinking about her now, I know she is with Jesus. You hear some "Christians" say that if you hear about Jesus once and deny him, there is no getting into heaven. Well, I don't believe that. Bree's father hurt her like mine did; she had no family and no fight, and I have to believe—no, I do believe—that Jesus is her daddy now and she is sitting with him.

I know the Jesus I now serve has compassion, and since Bree lived hell on earth, I believe when she died she went to heaven; Jesus was right there and grabbed her, and I am sure she sat in his arms and let him hold her. Just like the way Luis and Polly held me they day I told them I was doing porn, it was a pure love, a safe love.

I can perfectly picture Jesus doing that when Bree died. I'm sure she entered heaven and Jesus said, "You are my daughter."

Bree, if I could say anything to you, I would say: party it up in heaven. You deserve it. You're my family and I love you. Thank you for being my strength when I needed it. I never told you that because I was too busy hiding my emotions.

✝ ✝ ✝

I'm not sure how long I was in northern California. Maybe a month, maybe a few weeks; I can't tell you. My time there became a blur of being strung up, chained, beaten, almost drowned, and raped by people and machines, and the entire time it was filmed.

When it was time to leave, Evan said, "We're going to stay in a hotel for a little while so you can regain your strength and look a little better." They couldn't have me going through an airport looking beaten and frail. I can't tell you how long I was in the hotel; it was as long as it took for my visible bruises to fade.

On the flight home, all I could think about was Bree. When we got back to Sebastian's house, Sebastian looked at me and said, "I don't even need to say anything, do I?" I shook my head no. He wanted to make sure I did not say anything about Bree.

My time at Sebastian's was spent doing adult films and having private one-on-ones with whomever he wanted. The people who bought time with me to act out their sick, twisted fantasies were police officers, police chiefs, pastors, people who worked in children's church, politicians, and celebrities.

Sometimes Sebastian would tell me who they were, and sometimes they would brag about it themselves. It was a prize for Sebastian that these "very important" people wanted to meet with "his girls," and wanted to pay high dollars to have sex with porn stars in private.

Sebastian also started to work with another agency by the name of Porn Models. The owner, Julian, wanted to book me too, so I started to be bounced back and forth between their houses. Julian was a male porn star who wanted his own agency; Sebastian helped him achieve that.

Once they partnered up, my bookings doubled, and then tripled. I would do about two films a day, and then at night I would meet three or four people to do "privates." Each time was a worse rape, a worse beating, and my body began to depend on whatever drugs were given to me. I was living in hell with no way out.

Sebastian started to book me with bigger companies like Hustler and Playboy, as well as the same porn entertainment company that sent me to him in the first place.

When I started to get these bookings, I knew I was never getting out of the porn business, never getting away from Sebastian. These were the prime people of adult entertainment and Sebastian knew that these companies didn't just take anyone—they wanted me. I had no tattoos and looked like the girl next door; I looked like a normal girl, not a porn star.

I began to accept that this was my life: sex, drugs, murder, and money, and there was no escape.

† † †

After about a year, Sebastian started to let me and some of the other girls go out at night to the clubs. Of course, we always had someone with us, but he gave us some freedom. Maybe Sebastian knew we wouldn't dare say anything, and he was right. Blame it on Stockholm syndrome, stupidity, fear, or whatever, but in my mind these nights let me go out and drink and become normal for a second, or at least try to be normal. I thought normal for my age was drinking, drugs, sex, and boys.

By this time, Sebastian had hired a new driver by the name of Eli. He was very handsome and was always around me. He would say things like, "I'm going to take you away from here one day; we will run away and be free." It gave me hope that maybe this guy would get me out of Los Angles and away from Sebastian.

Looking back and thinking of all these different men I trusted over the years, I realize I was acting like my mom, trying to find the next man for my escape. Funny that now, as I write this, I don't want anything to with any man. Thinking about going on a date or thinking a guy is cute is a scary thing for me. I don't want what all those men were to me: someone who found a beautiful face to have sex with and abuse.

Eli and I did become close, or what I thought was close at the time. I thought closeness was sex, and when he wanted it I gave it to him. Sex to me was meaningless—it was normal for someone to want it from me, and it was normal for me to pretend I was having the time of my life during it. If I didn't pretend to enjoy myself, there were consequences from Sebastian; I would get beaten up or the sex would get harder and worse. I thought all men were like that.

Anytime I went out at night, Eli was there. He was my friend—or so I thought. I ultimately learned that the biggest mistake in the adult film industry is thinking anyone is your friend. But once, after a Hustler photo/video shoot, Eli took me to talk to Sebastian and Julian. He dropped me off and said, "I will come and get you later."

"What's going on?"

"I'll just come get you later," he said.

As soon as I walked in the house, Sebastian grabbed me, ripped off my clothes, a camera was put in my face, and I was raped by about fifteen men, including Julian. I can't tell you how long it lasted; I just know that when everyone was done I could not even walk because I was so sore.

"That was the best gang rape I've ever been a part of," Sebastian said.

There was another girl there with me, and when everything was done, she came and got me and said, "Come on." I couldn't walk, so Julian and Sebastian picked me up and put me in the bathtub.

I wanted to cry at that moment, I wanted to give up, I had no fight in me. How much more could I take? Rape, sodomy, broken trust, abuse... death is what I wanted. Death felt like the only option for me after that; I could not endure much more torture.

While I was in the bath, Sebastian and Julian came in. Sebastian said, "That was your last shoot in the United States." I didn't know what that meant, but it didn't sound good. "Eli is going to come and get you," he said. "Go with him to his house."

I had a blind hope that Eli had done something to get me out; in the back of my mind, that was the meaning behind "the last shoot in the United States."

When Eli came to pick me up, he had a couple of other girls in his car and said, "You are all coming with me." Before I got into the car Sebastian came out, grabbed me and kissed me.

"You were one of my most prized possessions," he said.

That was the last time I ever saw Sebastian.

"We're all going overseas tomorrow," Eli said, "so you'll all need a good night's rest."

"What?" I said.

"There are some very powerful, rich people who have bought each of you. You're going to go and live with them. They own you now."

My mind was racing. What? Is this how I'm going to die, overseas? What's going to happen? I was so scared. I was okay with death, but not like this.

Eli's house looked just like a normal house, but it had a built-in basement, and Eli took all of us down to it. If you know anything about California, you know that houses don't have basements unless people put one in themselves. This wasn't a basement—it was a prison cell.

I didn't sleep at all that night and when the morning came, I heard on the door a loud bang-bang-bang.

"Open the door!" came a voice. "Police! Open the door!"

"Yes?" came Eli's voice.

"I have a warrant for Madyson's arrest," said the police officer.

"There's no one by the name of Madyson here."

One of Eli's guys came down to the basement, grabbed me, and took me upstairs to hide in a closet.

"I have a warrant to search the premises," the officer said, "so either hand her over or I am searching the house."

Eli could not risk the police searching the house and finding the other girls, so he said, "She's hiding in the closet."

The officer opened the closet door, stuck his gun against my forehead, and said, "Let me see your hands! Get on the floor!"

I complied quickly.

"Are you stupid for hiding?" he said. "I could have shot you."

In my pajama pants, I was arrested.

The police never found those girls because I never told them.

To this day, I still don't know how the police knew I was there. I do wish at that moment of being handcuffed, I had said something about the basement and the other girls down there, but I didn't. I'd seen how corrupt police could be; I'd been bought by most of the higher-ups in local law enforcement, so I did not dare tell them.

Looking back, my heart breaks, because I could have changed the course of someone's life if I had just spoken up.

Instead, I just got arrested. It was one of the best things that happened to me.

† † †

Sheep In Wolves Clothing

Out Of the Darkness

I knew why I was being arrested. I'd done some complicated money switching when Adrian cut off our accounts. I still had blank checks from one account, so I had used one of those checks to open an account at another bank, writing the check for ten thousand dollars and receiving almost four thousand dollars in cash up front.

Naturally, the check bounced, the bank got the authorities involved, and I was charged with felony burglary. I was supposed to go to court, but I'd missed my court date because of Sebastian, and that led to the warrant.

I don't know how they found me. Sebastian and Julian supposedly had made my whereabouts untraceable, but the police still got to me.

I tried to lie to the officer. "I'm not Madyson!" I said. "Let me go! It's not me!" A part of me was scared about what Sebastian might do when he found out, what would he done to the people I loved and cared about. It didn't work.

I left with the police, and when we stopped in a grocery center to arrest someone else, the officer came up to me with somewhat compassionate eyes. "You are Madyson, aren't you?"

"Yes," I said, and I started to cry.

"Get out the car," he said softly. I did, and he removed my handcuffs from behind my back and cuffed me with my hands in front of me. It was a nice gesture, one I wasn't used to. "When we get close to the station, I'll have to put them back, though."

They made their other arrest and took me to the station. When I got there, I was so scared. It was gross and dirty; there were people coming off drugs and officers getting rough with people who were out of line. They sat me on a bench, in front of which was a lady and a sign that said REGISTRATION.

When you go to jail, the first thing you do is register and talk to a nurse to make sure you are not on any medication, pregnant, or anything of that sort. The lady asked me my name and whether I was on any medication, and then said, "How did you get those bruises on your arms and neck?"

I didn't respond.

"Are you okay? Do you need a doctor?"

I shook my head, and one of the officers standing behind her said, "Answer her with your words."

"No."

They put me in a concrete cell with only a toilet and a sink. The cell had clear walls, so anyone walking by could see me. I stayed there for a while until my name was called, and then I went into a little room. On one side was a woman who worked for the jail; on the other side was me.

"Do you know why you are here?" she said.

"Yes."

"We are not going to release you on your own recognizance. You also have some unpaid tickets, so your bail is set at one hundred thousand dollars. We're going to move you to a cell with a phone. Make your calls and see if you can make bail."

They moved me, but I did not have anyone's recent phone numbers memorized, so I could not get hold of anyone. I dialed at random, but nothing went through. Finally, I tried one last number: my father's.

He answered. I started to cry and told him my situation and begged him to bail me out.

"I don't have that kind of money," he said, "but if the bail was lower I would get you out." Funny that the only person I reached is the one person I hated most in life. I don't even know how I remembered his number for that long.

† † †

When you go to jail, you have to get processed before you get a bed, so you stay in this concrete cell anywhere from eight to ten hours. When it's time to get transferred into general population, you have to shower. You take off all your clothes in front of about ten women and three guards, and you have to wash your hair so they can make sure you aren't hiding anything. Then they give you a uniform: blue pants, white undershirt, blue shirt, socks, and orange shoes. They then give you a bed with sheets.

The next morning at five, the guards wake everyone up. You make your bed, then stand in front of your bunk while they do roll call. Once that is done, you have the option to go to breakfast. I didn't; I just got back in bed and cried. I only got out of bed when I was told to.

When the weekend came around, it was time for visitors. I didn't think I would have anyone, but lo and behold my name was called. When I went down to the visitor's section, standing there were my mom and my sister Ava.

Ava and I had been really close before I disappeared, and even to this day she has never judged me for anything I have done; she has just loved me and been a friend. Seeing her made me happy, but I didn't know what to think about seeing my mother. I did think, Of course my mother is here when something bad is happening, but she is never here when things are good.

When someone visits you in jail, there is a clear window that separates you and a phone on each side you use to communicate. I picked up the phone and my mom started to cry.

"Are you okay?" she said. "Do you need anything?"

"Can you bail me out?"

"The bail is too high right now, but if we can get that down then I will make your father bail you out. I am going to put some money on your books here so you can buy candy or coffee once a week. And we'll be at your court date on Monday."

Then she handed the phone to Ava and we talked only for a minute. She told me she loved me and was here for me, and she tried to make jokes and make me laugh, because that is just who she is. When someone she loves is hurting, she tries to make them smile.

Soon my time was up, and I went back to my dorm: concrete floors and walls surrounding approximately fifteen people. But that weekend, my name got called again by the guards, and they told me my lawyer was here.

Well, when a lawyer visits you, it's different. Instead of phones and glass, you go into a private room where you can actually touch the person. Well, when I walked in, I immediately recognized who was sitting there. It was a guy by the name of Tristan, the administrator for my previous school.

"Your mom asked me to come see you, since I'm a lawyer now."

I wanted to ask him if he was the new guy screwing my mom, but I didn't. Instead, there was a sense of relief that someone I knew was sitting in front of me, and I didn't really care who it was as long as it wasn't someone from the porn industry.

"I'm going to try and get your tickets as time served in Long Beach and that should reduce your bail," he said.

"Why are you doing this?" I said.

"I love your mom," he said, "and it's really hurting her that you are in here. I am going to do whatever I can do to help you. Do you need your mom?"

I thought about it for a moment. "Yes." I don't know why I said yes, because she had never been there for me before—unless she could make a spectacle of the bad things that were happening in her life and her kids' lives. But I said yes anyway.

We finished our meeting, and then a few hours later my name was called again and I was told once more that my lawyer was there. When I walked in, and saw who was sitting there, I broke down.

It was a man named Najar.

Najar was a law-school friend of my sister Charlotte. I'd met him before I made the choice to do porn, and he was like a brother. He loved me and wanted good for me; seeing him gave me such a sense of relief. When I finally pulled myself together, I said, "So I guess you passed the bar?" We just started laughing.

"I can't represent you because I am a public defender," he said, "but I wanted to make sure you were okay. I'll visit you once a week until you get out of here."

I unloaded on Najar and told him everything that had happened in the past few years. Then Najar told me he would coach Tristan on how to get my bail reduced and tickets in Long Beach as time served. Then our time was up and I went back to my cell.

I didn't think I was getting any more visitors, but my name was called again, and again I was told my lawyer was there to see me. This time it was Charlotte's ex-boyfriend Bruce, who was also a lawyer. He told me he loved me and would be there for me in whatever ways I needed, and that he was going to help Tristan as well.

As I made my way back to my cell, I heard one of the guards remark, "Wow, you're popular tonight."

†　†　†

Monday came around, and I was awakened extremely early to be transported by bus with other inmates to the courthouse. I went to court and was assigned a public defender, who advised me to plead not guilty.

On the way back to jail, the guard said, "I know you. I know who you are."

I didn't say anything.

"You're that porn star," he said. "You're Fayth."

"No, you're wrong," I said.

He laid his hand on my leg said, "I'm a huge fan of your work."

I was disgusted and wanted him to take his hand off me, but I didn't know what would happen if I told him to.

The next few weeks in jail were hell. At night, my name would be called, and I would be taken to the roof. There, the guards would have their way with me; I was raped over and over on the rooftop. The majority of the time it was that one guard, but there were others.

After about forty-five days inside, I noticed this girl who worked at the jail. I saw her from far away but I knew that I knew her, I just couldn't remember how. Almost every day, they would give the inmates the option of going to the roof to get outside, but I never wanted to go because of what was happening.

One day they made the call for people who wanted to go the roof. An inmate who was in my dorm said, "You want to come outside?"

"No."

"Skylar wants you to come to the roof."

That's who that is! Skylar, Tristan's daughter. I knew her well because she had been Charlotte's best friend in school. Skylar was always very skinny and kind of frail-looking, with short blonde hair and light eyes.

I went up to the roof and met Skylar. I started to cry again. "I want out of here," I said.

"My father's gotten the parking tickets as time served," she said, "and now your bail is down to fifty thousand."

"That's still high," I said.

"Well, maybe the public defender can get the bail reduced."

"Skylar, do you know what happens here at night?"

Her eyes got wide. "No. No, and don't tell me." She knew. She just did not want the responsibility of being told about it.

That night one girl in my dorm looked at me and said, "You think you're so pretty and cute."

"No, I don't."

"Yes, you do."

Then she jumped me and started beating away on me.

The dorm had an alarm you could pull in an emergency, and someone pulled it. The guards came in and broke up the fight, then announced they were transferring me into another dorm.

While the guard was walking me to the other dorm, she said, "If people ask why you were transferred, tell them you beat up another girl."

† † †

That weekend, Charlotte, Sophie, and my father all visited me. Charlotte got on the phone first and the first thing out of her mouth was, "How are you able to be so beautiful in a place like this?"

"Huh?"

"It's gross here but you look so beautiful!" she said. "Anyway, I've spoken with Sebastian and I'm going to get some money from him to bail you out."

"What?"

"He owes you money, right?"

"No, he doesn't," I said. "Don't call him again, don't get money from him."

She didn't say anything; she just passed the phone to my father.

"How are you doing?" he said.

"You need to bail me out," I said. "You owe me. I just got beaten up." I don't know why I told him he owed me; maybe I wanted him to know that I knew the pain he'd caused me as a little girl wasn't okay.

"I'm trying my hardest," he said, and then he passed the phone to Sophie, whom I had not seen since I last tried to get help from her. She started quoting all these Bible verses and I wanted to tell her to shut up, I wanted to throw up, I didn't care what her Jesus had to say, and I didn't care what came out of her Bible.

She then said, "I want Samantha and Truth to visit you. I'm going to bring them to visit you." Samantha and Truth were her kids, my niece and nephew.

"What?" I said. "No, I don't want them to see me in here. Jail is not a place for a kids." Is she on crack? I thought. What is wrong with her?

She just got mad and said, "Fine."

Then they left, and I went back to my dorm, going on seventy-one days in jail. I was done. Ready to give up. I could not take it anymore. My family were whack jobs, and the fact that my sister Charlotte was in communication with Sebastian made me think I was dead already.

I got up to use the restroom and saw a woman watching me.

"Hey, you," she said.

I ignored her, but she got up and said, "Hey you. I'm talking to you. Do you know why I am in here?"

"No."

"I'm in jail for seven days for driving on a suspended license," she said. "You're Madyson, right?"

"Yes."

"Madyson, tomorrow you will be getting out of jail. Jesus told me."

I just looked at her and laughed. "Jesus doesn't exist," I said.

I'd heard of stories of people who had committed suicide in jail, so I was ready. I was done. Time to say goodbye to life. Death had to be better than the hell I'd been living for the past few years, better than the hell I was living at that moment.

The following morning, while the guards did roll call, I lay in bed thinking of how I could do it. I can hang myself with a sheet, but I should do that at night. I can ask someone to kill me who's already been sentenced to life. Ideas ran through my head. I didn't know how, but I knew I was going to die that day.

When you're in general population of a jail, you have a room attached to your dorm with a TV, some benches, and metal tables and chairs. As I was plotting my suicide in my head, I heard a really loud sound coming from the TV in that room. My first thought was that someone was going to be in trouble for having the TV that loud, but the volume just got louder and louder until I recognized it.

It was a song. It was the song. "Come Just As You Are," the song I had heard Crystal Lewis sing as a little girl.

"Come just as you are. Hear the Spirit call."

I got out of bed and went into the TV room. There was a choir singing on the screen, and then a pastor named Joel Osteen came on and started talking.

"You are in the darkest place you have ever been, you are ready to give up, you are ready to die, but listen to me right now: don't kill yourself, don't give up. Jesus loves you and he is saying at this moment, 'Come just as you are, come just as you are.'"

As he talked, tears streamed down my face. I looked to the ceiling and whispered, "Okay, Jesus. You get one last chance with me. Don't f*** it up. I won't take my life now; it's yours."

I don't know why I trusted God at that moment. I guess that song took me back to when I was a little girl at Fashions of Each Era with Crystal Lewis, Peyton, Sophie's friend Harper, and my sisters. I was happy and I had a belief deep down that Jesus was real. After that prayer, I sensed that everything was going to be okay. I think God was starting to piece me back together and giving me the little bit of peace I needed.

† † †

About an hour later, my name was called and I thought, It's not a day for visitors; maybe Najar or Tristan or Bruce is here. I started to go to the door but a guard stopped me. "Go get your bed."

Huh?

"You're getting out of here," one of the inmates said. "Go get your bed."

Did that inmate last night give me a prophecy? Am I really getting out of here?

I didn't believe it, but sure enough, I was processed out, and when I walked out the door my mother and Charlotte were standing there. They hugged me and said, "Let's get you home."

On the drive to my mother's apartment, I rolled the window down and stuck my head out all the way. It was the first time in a long time I wasn't in some type of bondage, and I just wanted to enjoy the moment.

When we arrived, I showered for what seemed like an hour. Charlotte lived with my mother after having a child and going through a divorce. After my shower, Charlotte gave me some clothes and then I piled in the bed with her and my niece Jayden, and we went to sleep.

I don't know how late I slept, but when I woke up my sister Ava was there, and she and my mom invited me out to breakfast. I think I ordered everything on the menu—it was like I hadn't eaten in years.

"You can stay with me throughout your court dates," my mother said, "but you need to find a job and pay some rent."

A job? What skills did I have besides having sex and being beaten up? Nevertheless, I started applying and found a job at a mortgage company cold-calling people. I didn't have any people skills, so it was hard, but it was something. It was an honest job.

† † †

Adjusting to Civilian Life

Though I was living with my mother, I was enjoying life and freedom for the time being. I would sit out by her pool when I wasn't working or walk around to the shops by her house. I knew life could be taken away again at any moment, because the maximum sentence for my crime was five years in prison. I still had in the back of my head that Charlotte was in contact with Sebastian, but I didn't care; I just enjoyed the moments of freedom I had.

Everyone in my family seemed to really be trying to make an effort with me. Sophie started taking me to a small church that met in a library close to my mother's house led by a man by the name of Pastor Joseph. It was actually sweet of her, since she had to drive from LA to Orange County every Sunday morning to go with me to church, then drive to LA and go to her church, Calvary Chapel. I just wasn't sure if she was coming because she cared about me, or if she was trying to slap my mom in the face.

Apparently Pastor Joseph was some sort of big music producer, but he was also someone who had been convicted of buying prostitutes after being arrested in a sting operation. I didn't find this out until later, and I don't know why Sophie would take me to a church led by someone with a history like that. In her defense, though, she didn't know the details of the hell I had been through because I never talked about it. She only knew the beginning of it, and since she didn't help me when I asked her to, I had no desire to explain what I had gone through.

My faith was still faltering. I believed, but didn't. I didn't know who Jesus really was, but I wanted to figure it out on my own. I didn't care for Sophie's Jesus.

I was also trying to adjust to normal civilian life (in the porn industry, you refer to everyone who is not in porn as a "civilian"). I had so much hanging over my head and wanted to escape so badly.

I once went to a night service at Pastor Joseph's because I was trying to get involved. I had been taught to walk into a room so confidently that everyone noticed, even if I was so shattered I thought I was beyond repair. If people saw confidence first, then they wouldn't see how broken I was. So I walked in to the sanctuary like I was the most beautiful person in the world, like I did not care who saw me, and with the attitude that if people wanted to get to know me, they needed to come to me first.

How sad, right?

Well, as I walked up, there were a couple of people talking. One was a guy named Tyler. I knew who he was because Sophie had mentioned him and his roommate Mark before; they worked together with Sophie and her best friend Harper with their non-profit organization helping woman and children in Africa.

Well, Tyler saw me come up and, just like me, he acted as if he owned the room.

"You must be Madyson," he said. "I'm Tyler. I know your sister Sophie."

He was disgustingly cocky, and in response I was kind of rude—but he also looked at me like a person, not a piece of meat, and that was refreshing. Later on, I discovered he was the guy at church that all the girls had a crush on; he certainly wasn't used to girls being jerks back to him.

So here I was, hating all men and not being particularly nice to him, which was something he wasn't too sure about or used to. Nevertheless, he pushed to become my friend, and eventually it worked. Every time I would go to church, he would talk to me; he got my number and called me all the time, though half the time I would ignore him. Finally, I allowed myself to open up a little bit, and Tyler became my friend.

I think Sophie hoped Tyler and I would get married and live happily ever after, but I never thought of Tyler like that. I didn't have those sorts of plans for us; I didn't even have a crush on him. It was just refreshing to hang out with a guy who wasn't trying to have sex with me.

It was refreshing to have a friend, even though I didn't know how to be a friend at that time (and kind of still don't!). Tyler and I hung out and talked on the phone. He urged me to enroll in school, which was frustrating for me, because I don't think he realized I was facing prison time.

Tyler was not used to me not wanting to date him. See, this church was very small, and all the "church" girls who had attended for years had walked a straight line their entire life. The next step on that straight line, their dream, was to get married to a "godly" man like Tyler and have a perfect life. Though I thought that life that didn't exist, it was their dream, and who was I to judge that? So after I would hang out with Tyler, some of the church girls would frequently jump on the opportunity to interrogate me, feeding their crushes on him.

I did want to have some girlfriends, so I became friends with two girls, Violet and Julia. Violet was shorter, thin, with white-blonde hair and light eyes, while Julia was the same height with red hair and freckles. Needless to say, they were not the typical girls I thought I would become friends with. Their dream was to get married; mine was to not go to prison.

When we hung out, they never asked me things like, "How are you doing? What's going on in your life? Do you need prayer for anything?" No, it was "How is hanging out with Tyler? Are you guys dating? Do you like him? Where do you guys go?"

One night, Julia came to pick me up for a Bible study "life group." It took some convincing to get me to come. Going to those things gave me a lot of anxiety because of what had happened at the Radiant Church life group, when they'd put my porn video in, but I agreed. I always feared someone was going to take me to one of these things and put in another video of me, or even worse—Sebastian would show up.

Julia picked me up from my mom's house, and as we drove, she started asking me a lot of questions about Tyler and his roommate, Mark. I started to feel uncomfortable, so I said, "Why do you keep asking me questions about these guys?"

This didn't feel like other times when I thought they were just being gossipy girls—it was like she was trying to get information out of me. See, when I got arrested, they interrogated me to see what I might say, and this felt a little like that.

"Tyler and Mark have a high calling," she said. "They're both called to be in ministry and be pastors."

What a horrible calling, I thought. Pastors were still evil in my mind, and Tyler and Mark were not evil guys, they just weren't.

"I Googled your name," she said, "and the pictures that came up were inappropriate and would ruin any ministry Tyler and Mark might have."

Those are just normal modeling pictures, I thought. It's not even porn.

Regardless, I wasn't going to go another mile with this woman.

"Pull the car over," I said. As I got out, I told her, "I don't want or need friends like you. And maybe you should let Mark and Tyler know what their calling is, because I don't think God has told them yet."

I already knew Tyler's heart was in missions because that's where he came from. Tyler had grown up in Africa with his missionary parents. Mark, on the other hand, had a suspicion his dad was former CIA, but they never talked about it. They wanted to follow their own dreams, not lead a church, and maybe that's why I liked them so much. They weren't pastors.

Before I go on: girls, you are not defined by whether you are married or not. You are also not defined by who you marry. If you are around people who make you feel as if you're incomplete without marriage, or you are in a church that pushes you that way, then leave those friends behind and find a new church, because God wants us to be happy, not to live for a man.

I had been defined by Adrian, then defined by the men in the porn industry. Marriage is a good thing, but even when you have a partner, you are not that partner. You are your own individual person, even when you're married. That person is your friend and partner, and that's it.

After I got out of Julia's car and started to walk home, I cried and cried. My thoughts were confused. I didn't understand what was going on, and I didn't understand why I had chosen the wrong friends again. I also didn't understand why I couldn't be a pastor's wife or in ministry.

God, why do you keep allowing people to mentally beat me up?

My faith was starting to be rocked in a major way, and at this point in my life, after everything I'd gone through, anything could have pushed me to not believe. But Tyler kept me believing; he was truly a pure, godly man who innocently wanted to be my friend.

† † †

At this time, I was going through so much: the progress of my court case, living with a mother I hadn't spoken to in years, and hanging out with the sisters I had long ago lost touch with… It was all so overwhelming. I wanted an escape. I constantly wanted to be somewhere different, living a different life.

When I was married to Adrian, I had created a Facebook account and was always on there browsing, looking at everyone's lives and how they were so different from mine. I decided to get back on, and it was fun, especially since I hadn't been on for years.

In the past, I'd connected with a lot of modeling pages (not porn, just fashion pages), and so I got random friend requests from people. At first I was very cautious, because I did not want Sebastian, Evan, Julian or anyone in the porn industry to find me.

The day Julia told me basically how horrible I was, I got a friend request from some random guy. At that point, I didn't care if Sebastian or anyone else found me—I didn't care about my life or see any value in it. The idea of prison held over my head felt like the end; it was either sex for money for Sebastian or prison. Anyway, this guy Charlie added me as a friend. In his profile picture he looked very handsome. like a model.

We became friends first on Facebook, and then we started emailing before eventually talking over the phone. The first time I heard his voice, I melted just a little at his sexy British accent. It was the escape I thought I needed. I mean, he was from another country and didn't know me or what I was going through.

Meanwhile, court was starting to become really intense as we prepared to go to trial. Life overall was also intense, and the novelty living with my mother had worn off. Things were not good. I was so confused, in need of a break from life, and that came when Charlie called me and invited me to visit him in London.

I didn't even consider whether I should or should not go—the answer was yes. London? Why would I think twice about that?

But how would I get there? The mortgage company I'd been working for had closed down, so I had no job. I was facing jail time. I just needed to figure out how I could make some money.

So I started looking for jobs on Craigslist. I still wanted to model, and there was a section on there for "models" with an ad that talked about making three hundred dollars in an hour. So I emailed and said I would like to model. Someone emailed me back with a phone number. I didn't think anything of it, so I called the number and arranged a meeting at a restaurant near my mother's house.

Chris was young, short, and fat, with black hair. When I saw him in that restaurant, I immediately thought he was kind of seedy-looking. I knew this wasn't going to be good, but I stayed to listen and see what he had to say.

"So you want to make money?" he said.

"Yes," I said.

"Wait—do I know you?"

"Excuse me?"

"You're that porn star!" he said.

Oh, great.

"This is great," he said, "you can make a lot of money."

I didn't really know how my porn background would help me make a lot of money as a fashion model—or maybe I did, but I just didn't want to let my mind go there.

"I'll pick you up tonight at eight," he said, and for some reason, I agreed. I did not ask why or what we were doing, I just said okay.

† † †

Chris picked me up on time and drove me to Los Angeles—a place I never wanted to see again—and said, "I found some good pictures of you." They were some modeling pictures as well as porn pictures. "Okay, now time to post the ad," he said.

I still did not ask for what.

I knew that I was back where I started.

I was about to go have sex with a stranger for three hundred dollars for the hour.

I knew deep down that it was prostitution. I'd been in a situation just like this before with Sebastian's driver.

You may be wondering why I would go through with this again. Why? Because there was a strange comfort in being there again—it was all I knew. It was something I was good at, or at least pretended to be. I missed it because it had been my life.

I don't miss it now, but at that moment in Chris's car, even though I was scared, I was a little bit relieved to be sitting there.

What else did I know how to do?

He used his phone to post an ad on Craigslist, and we started to receive calls right away. Meanwhile, he instructed me how to spot the cops and their sting operations. We always had the phone on speaker, and when calls came in Chris told me to accept them or hang up if he thought they were cops. He then gave me condoms and took me to the first house.

I could not believe this was happening.

When I was done at the first house, I walked back to the car, where Chris waited outside for me.

"Did you get the money?"

I showed him. "Yeah."

"Give me one hundred and fifty. This is how our relationship will work. You go on the appointment, collect the money and give me half."

I did it. I did not fight and I did not ask why. I just did it.

When Chris said he was picking me up, I went with him.

Very soon I had enough money to go to London.

† † †

I connected with Charlie and bought my ticket to travel to London for a few days. Charlie told me he would pay for everything else I needed while in London: food, liquor, the works.

My flight was uneventful, but when I got off the plane, Charlie wasn't there to meet me. I didn't know what to do. And then I had a horrible thought: What if this was a setup all along, and London was where Sebastian had been planning to send me?

I don't know why I wasn't scared flying over there, but at the moment when I didn't see Charlie, I became terrified.

And then, peeking out of the crowd, I saw a guy who was so handsome. He looked at me and said, "Madyson?"

"Charlie?"

It was him.

He hugged me and said, "Wow, you are so beautiful." It was a perfect, romantic moment in London.

We got on the train, went back to his flat to drop off my stuff, and then spent a romantic few days in London. I got lost in it. I had so much on my plate at home, and now I was in a different country with a guy who hardly knew me but didn't care... it was perfect, and I didn't want it to end.

When it was time to go home, Charlie asked me to come back again, this time to live there with him. It was the perfect escape: run from the court, run from Chris, run from my mom, run from the porn industry that was haunting me and live in London with Charlie.

"We'll see," I said and got on the plane home.

† † †

That following Monday was another court date, and I just wanted it to end. Every night before court, my mom wanted me to stay home at her house, while Sophie wanted me to spend the night at her house. Whomever I chose, the other one was mad at me. It was exhausting, and I was sick of the tug of war, so I switched off every other court date just to make it fair.

This time it was Sophie's turn. As she drove me to her place, she asked me if I had my Bible with me.

"Yes," I said, thinking, *Here we go again with the Bible. Is this going to get me out of court?* It was late, so we went to bed when we arrived. I lay down on the white couch in her living room, covered myself with her purple blanket, and stared at the ceiling.

Decorating their living room was this curiosity: a Jesus face made from straw, which I could see straight on from my position on the couch. At first, I thought, Who wants a creepy Jesus face in their house? And then I noticed my Bible lying there, and it honestly looked like the creepy Jesus was staring at me, telling me to pick up my Bible. Since I was too stressed out about court to sleep, I picked up my blue, New Living Translation of the Bible, turned on the light, and opened it up.

I didn't know what I was looking for, so I just opened it and read the first thing I saw. It was Psalm 32. As I read this chapter, I started to really think about my life, what I had done, the lies I had told... It was very fitting of God to allow me to read this right before court. Here is what this chapter states:

> Oh, what joy for those
>   whose disobedience is forgiven,
>   whose sin is put out of sight!
> Yes, what joy for those
>   whose record the Lord has cleared of guilt,
>   whose lives are lived in complete honesty!

When I refused to confess my sin,
> my body wasted away,
> and I groaned all day long.

Day and night your hand of discipline was heavy on me.
> My strength evaporated like water in the summer heat...

Finally, I confessed all my sins to you
> and stopped trying to hide my guilt.

I said to myself, "I will confess my rebellion to the Lord."
> And you forgave me! All my guilt is gone...

Therefore, let all the godly pray to you while there is still time,
> that they may not drown in the floodwaters of judgment.

For you are my hiding place;
> you protect me from trouble.
> You surround me with songs of victory...

The Lord says, "I will guide you along the best pathway for your life.
> I will advise you and watch over you.

Do not be like a senseless horse or mule
> that needs a bit and bridle to keep it under control."

Many sorrows come to the wicked,
> but unfailing love surrounds those who trust the Lord.

So rejoice in the Lord and be glad, all you who obey him!

Shout for joy, all you whose hearts are pure!

Verse 5 affected me especially strongly: "Finally, I confessed all my sins to you and stopped trying to hide my guilt. I said to myself, 'I will confess my rebellion to the Lord,' and you forgave me! All my guilt is gone."

I read this over and over again, and I quietly started to cry (with creepy Jesus still staring at me), and I said, "Jesus, help... I need help. I'm trapped."

I felt I had been trapped in this life I didn't want, this life full of sins for which I needed forgiveness: forgiveness for stealing from the bank, forgiveness for the choices I had made, and forgiveness from the people I had hurt.

So after praying and crying, I said to myself, I am going into court tomorrow and I am pleading guilty.

† † †

I didn't tell my family. I think I didn't tell them because I didn't want them to attempt to influence my choice of plea, and frankly, I just didn't want their input. I felt like for the first time in my life, I was allowing God to speak to me, and I was hearing his voice.

I wanted to be obedient. It wasn't everyone else's "Jesus" telling me to do something; it really was Jesus, speaking sweetly to me. It was me believing for the first time in a long time, and it was me allowing Jesus to speak with me.

That morning I made one phone call, to Najar.

"I want to plead guilty."

"You're crazy," he said.

"But I am guilty," I said. "My public defender has, like, a hundred cases, and I'm not a priority, so how do I plead guilty without driving her crazy?"

He told me how to do it. When my name was called to stand in front of the court that day, my attorney and I approached the bench, and she said, "Your Honor, we would like to request a continuance."

The judge started to look at his calendar, and I interrupted.

"Your Honor," I said, "no disrespect, but may I please say something?" The judge looked at my attorney and she was baffled, along with my mother, sister, and brother-in-law, but I just kept looking at the judge

"Go ahead," he said.

"Your Honor, I know you have many people who come up here and claim their innocence. Well, I am not innocent. I did commit these crimes, and I would like to change my plea from not guilty to guilty."

My attorney immediately interrupted. "My client does not know what she is saying. She is not competent."

"Your honor," I said, "I would like to let go of my counsel and plead guilty."

The judge looked at me and said, "Maybe you should listen to your attorney."

"Your Honor, if I am not able to get rid of my counsel, then I would like to call a Marsden motion." Najar had told me to say that. A Marsden motion is when you want to fire your attorney while in front of the judge and the judge will not allow you. Your case then goes on hold and you immediately go into another courtroom with another judge and your attorney. This other judge will then decide if you are competent at that time to fire your attorney.

We adjourned for the Marsden motion, and my family was livid. I think they were angry because I made the choice on my very own to plead guilty, and they had no control over it. They also couldn't be in the courtroom during the Marsden motion, so they were upset that they couldn't see the drama unfold. I didn't care; I just wanted to plead guilty, serve my time and be done with it.

Once in this other courtroom, the judge asked me, "What is your reason for wanting to fire your attorney?"

I had the verse written on my hand and I read it aloud: "Finally, I confessed all my sins to you and stopped trying to hide my guilt. I said to myself, 'I will confess my rebellion to the Lord.' And you forgave me! All my guilt is gone."

I looked at the judge and started to cry. "Your Honor, I know you have a lot of people who claim they're innocent, who want to fight when they're guilty." And then I told her what had happened the night before with my Bible, looked at my hand, read the verse again, and said, "Your Honor, I'm guilty. I just want to admit my guilt."

She looked at me, looked at my attorney, was quiet for a moment, and then said, in a choked-up voice, "Please give me a minute."

She then looked at me and said, "Young lady, I have been in the legal system for over twenty years and never in my life have I seen someone wanting to admit their guilt as much as you; it's refreshing that you want to be honest. We don't see that. Ever. After you are done with these hearings, you will do great things as long as you keep that thought process." She paused. "Will you please do me one thing?"

"Of course, Your Honor."

"Please read to me again that verse you have written on your hand."

I read it to her and suddenly a tear rolled down her face. Everything in this moment seemed to be happening in slow motion. I looked at my public defender as the judge said, "I am about to say something a judge should never say: Madyson, if I could, I would give you a hug." Then she looked at my public defender. "I am not allowing this young lady to plead guilty; I expect you to give her the best legal defense you can."

I thought, Great, I'm stuck with this pissed-off attorney.

Now it was time to go into pre-trial, which is a trial with another judge who decides whether there is enough evidence to go to a jury trial. We rushed into a third courtroom and started. My family was there waiting for the drama to unfold. They were unsure what had happened in the Marsden motion, but they could see I had not been able to fire my attorney.

We went into that third courtroom, and my attorney was a shark. She interrogated anyone who testified against me and made them seem like they didn't know what they were talking about.

After about fifteen minutes and only two witnesses, this third judge addressed the district attorney. "You do not have enough to pursue these charges." She banged her gavel. "Dismissed!"

I did not understand. "What is going on?" I said to my attorney. "What is happening?"

"We won this round, kid," she said. "Only a few more to go."

See, these were not all the charges against me, but to have these dismissed was huge.

"Now the rest of your case will be transferred to another court and you will get a new public defender," she said, starting to walk away, then stopping and turning around. "I will never forget you, kid."

I didn't know if that was a good thing or not. I didn't care. I just smiled and thought, Wow, Jesus really did take care of me. I obeyed him and he had my back.

My charges had been dropped in Newport Beach, CA, and now the remaining cases were transferred to Santa Ana Court, the big courthouse in Orange County.

† † †

Adjusting to Civilian Life

My Fathers Daughter

A Romantic Distraction

After all this, I started to feel God's presence become real in my life. I knew I could never see Chris again, but I really wanted to see Charlie again. Chris tried to call me, but I told him to leave me alone, that I wasn't doing that anymore. I suddenly had this power in me that was...that was... I know what it was: I started to have a voice and was learning to use it.

Charlie flew out to LA to see me, and he invited me to London again. I told him I would come, but that I needed to take care of some things at home first.

Then I told him what was going on.

I told him about the porn industry, about what I was going through in the court system... I told him everything. Afterward, he said I just needed to move to London to escape everything I was going through. I told him I wasn't going to move, but I promised to visit him again.

I finally went to my last court hearing and told my new public defender that I wanted to plead guilty. She was a little shocked, but she was eventually able to work out a deal with the district attorney where I could be on house arrest or spend six months in jail.

Once I took the deal, there was a long period of time— about six months—before I had to go to court and formally plead guilty. I was excited, because that meant I got to spend some extended time with Charlie in London.

When I was sitting in the airport waiting for my flight to leave for London, Tyler called me and asked me what I was doing.

I told him about my trip and about Charlie.

"Oh, I'm on my way to the airport to pick up Mark," he said. Then he begged me not to get on the plane but instead to go home with him and Mark.

I told him I wanted to go to London, but Tyler begged and pleaded with me not to. I didn't listen. That was the last night I talked to Tyler; we've just lost touch since then. I know Sophie wanted me to marry Tyler, but I'm glad I didn't. He wasn't the one God had chosen for me—God chose him to be a friend in a very difficult time in my life, and that was it.

So I flew off to London, this magical place of romance. I pretended everything was normal while I was there, that I belonged in this different country and was in love. It didn't matter where I had been; in this amazing city, I was a new person.

I told Charlie that I would only be staying for a few weeks and then I needed to go back home to start my house arrest. Or jail. He wanted me to stay in London forever, so he proposed to me.

I was in shock. In my heart, I didn't want to get married, because I was still in pain from the way Adrian had broken my heart.

But I still said yes.

I think I was caught up in the moment, but deep down I knew I didn't love this guy—I loved the city. It was London. How do you not fall "in love," or what you think is love, in London?

I stayed up all night, sitting on a bench attached to his window, staring into the sky. Why didn't I say no? I was so used to giving men what they wanted that I just complied.

Charlie wanted us to live in Los Angeles. I was okay with that, because I needed to get my house arrest over with, so we flew back to LA, got married, and moved into my mom's apartment. I didn't want a wedding; I just wanted a justice of the peace to marry us, so that's what we did.

After a few days of being married, Charlie told me he only married me because he wanted legal status in the United States. I was pissed. I told him he had two choices: he could pay me a certain amount of money to stay married to me, or we could get a divorce. I told him if he wanted a business transaction, then he could have that, but he was going to pay me to keep his residency.

"I don't have that kind of money," he said.

"Then we're getting divorced."

A couple of days later I went to the courthouse and found some attorneys who help people with divorce cases. I explained the situation and they said, "Well, you don't need to get a divorce; you've only been married for seven days and can get it annulled."

I filed annulment papers and things went from bad to worse.

Charlie called my sister Bella, saying that I had lied to him and asking why she didn't warn him. Bella just made things worse, and then everything felt like it was piling up to a point where I couldn't handle it anymore.

My mother had some sleeping pills at her house, so I took the entire bottle in an attempt to end my life. It didn't do anything but make me really sick. When my mother found me at her house, she said I needed to get out because her boyfriend was coming over and she had decided to get married. She told me I needed to go find my husband.

I walked out and sat at the top of her apartment stairs. There were these two guys who lived across the way whom I would hang out with from time to time. They saw me just sitting there and invited me over to their house, where I told them my entire sob story. They let me stay at their house for a few days until I figured something else out. It sure beat the streets.

†　†　†

My Father's Daughter

8

the Real Jesus

Throughout all of this, I was in contact with Peyton. She had told me I could stay with her during my house arrest. Well, when I called her crying from those guys' apartment, she said she was coming to get me.

I still didn't know if I was going to be able to do house arrest or if I would have to go to jail. I was planning to take the six months in jail; with house arrest, you need to pay a fee, and I was broke and alone and couldn't afford it.

"God will work it out," Peyton said as she drove me to her house in Irvine. I walked in, and everything was so clean and put in its place just right. Her father, Papa J, was there; I vaguely remembered him from when I was little. My main memory was that he was always cooking. He gave me a hug, which took me back a little.

"Go upstairs," Peyton said. "You can stay in Riley's room." That was her teenage son. She had the room already prepared for me like she knew I was coming, so I went upstairs and settled my stuff. I felt a little weird, like I was imposing on her, but she was so gracious, making sure I ate well and was comfortable.

About a week later, I had my sentencing hearing and the court told me I had two weeks to check in for either house arrest or jail.

"Well, I told Peyton, "I will probably just go to jail."

"No, you don't have to go to jail," she said. "You're going to do house arrest. God will work it out."

At this point, my belief was not so strong. But though it was little, it was still there.

A few days, later Peyton told me someone had donated the first installment for my house arrest to Fashion of Each Era Ministries, and she took me to register for house arrest. Before you can start, you have to go to the jail, check in, and get processed. It takes about eight hours, and you have to wait in a jail cell to be processed.

As I was being processed, another girl was being defiant, so one officer said, "Well, let's wait to release them." The officers could hold you as long as they wanted for processing. Another officer said, "No, Madyson is listening with the rest of the girls; let's just let them go."

They let us go, but my house arrest hadn't officially started.

Peyton picked me up at the jail. "We're going to church," she said.

Church? She is going to take me to church? Why?

"I'm going to take you to Radiant Church," she said.

I freaked out. "I am not going there," I said. "Please, anywhere but there." Peyton didn't know how those pastors had treated me; she just wanted to take me to church.

She ended up taking me to a church called the Sanctuary, which was filled with people who had gotten off of drugs or just gotten out of prison; you could tell everyone felt broken and just wanting something, anything, a glimpse of hope. But I felt a peace there, and I felt safe.

I think I felt safe because everyone in there was just as broken as me, and the preaching style reminded me of the apostolic church. I guess I felt comfortable around other broken people because I was so shattered myself.

A few days later my house arrest officially started. They gave me my ankle bracelet, I took a drug test, and they explained the rules explained to me. I was allowed to go look for a job during certain hours of the day, and once I found a job I had to check in with my case officer and let him know my schedule.

† † †

I found a job within walking distance from Peyton's house as a hostess and server at On the Border Mexican Grill, and I worked as much I could. I didn't want to think about house arrest, and I didn't want to be stuck in the house; the only way to feel free was to work all the time.

Papa J made sure to pick me up at night; he was concerned for me when I walked home late. He would also take me to church on Sundays, because during house arrest you were allowed to have two hours of worship each week. Anyone who knew Papa J knew that he was a servant, and he served me; he took me to church and to see my probation officer, he picked me up from work, and he drove me to work.

Papa J and I got really close, and he became the grandpa I never had. He loved me and I loved him, and it was a pure love.

Papa J was also close with Sophie, but he told me, "I love your sister, but I love you more." Then he would whisper, "You need a pure love more than Sophie."

I think he meant that I had been so broken and needed some pure love in my life, and Sophie had her husband for that, but I don't know for sure. I never got a chance to ask him—he passed away before I could. I think God kept him here on earth because I was the last person he was supposed to serve. He had a servant's heart, and it showed in the way he served me. I miss him very much, but he has a huge piece of my heart.

† † †

It was a little awkward moving in with Peyton. She still had two kids at home and was going through a lot in her household, but she brought me in. Her marriage was struggling, her kids were hitting puberty, and her body was going through some changes as she aged that made her off balance a lot of the time.

Sophie also got mad at Peyton for bringing me into her house; Sophie thought I needed to sit in jail for six months. She thought I needed to be truly punished. But Peyton disagreed.

She said God told her to bring me into her home and thank God, thank God Peyton listened to the Lord's voice.

I was able to find myself during that house arrest. In the mornings when I got up, Peyton's husband was at work and her kids were involved in their summer activities, so a lot of the time it was just me and Peyton. I would go into Peyton's room first thing in the morning. She always had her Bible open, her journal open, and Joyce Meyer or another preacher on the TV. She would share with me what she was reading or studying.

For a few weeks I just listened, then I started to ask questions and even argue about what she was telling me, not believing that her Jesus was real. But eventually I started to open up to her. I knew that, whatever I told her, she wasn't going to judge me, although I was afraid to talk about the porn. She never asked me about it, which was unusual; when someone finds out you did adult films, they usually have a million questions to ask you.

She didn't, though. She just waited for me to open up to her. Peyton simply loved me. Peyton is also a peacemaker, so she wanted me to talk to my mother and Sophie, but I was in a place where I didn't want to talk to them, didn't want anything to do with them.

I wanted to get to know Madyson.

I wanted to know who I was, and I couldn't do that with everyone in my ear telling me who I should be.

Peyton had a sister named Sadie who also loved me. She would come over and I would talk with her, and she understood how I felt about my family. She let me vent because she understood. We related to each other because we were both the babies in our family, and our voices were never really heard.

Sadie and I also had a different perception of who Jesus was than all those around us did. Everyone around us was legalistic, with these specific rules dictating who Jesus was, and Sadie and I simply believed Jesus loved us, shattered and all. It was a special bond she and I had.

During my house arrest, I hung out with Sadie, her ex-husband Blake, Peyton and her husband Ian, and of course Papa J. They had their issues (what family doesn't?), but they all loved me and understood what I was going through. They all gave me different advice, but never once judged me.

While living with Peyton I got a new Bible, and every morning I would say, "Okay, God, here is my question..." I would ask a question, then open up the Bible and each time find an answer or a promise from God. I started to share with Peyton and Peyton would said, "God knows how to speak to you."

I started to believe it.

And then I started to have dreams.

Now, prophecy is something you may not believe in, but I sure do. It was something that confused me at first, but I journaled about my dreams and didn't tell anyone. I did eventually start to talk with Peyton about God speaking to me, and then I started to open up about the porn industry, and then about Adrian. I guess I missed him, missed my bond with him. I was also devastated that I had hurt his parents the way I did.

Peyton would always listen, never judging, then give me the advice she thought was right. She would ask me if I thought Adrian and I would ever get back together, but I told her I knew Adrian wasn't the one God chose for me; he was the one I chose to get out of a bad situation.

†　†　†

House arrest lasted all summer, and it wasn't long before it came to an end and it was time to have that ankle bracelet removed. I had been in bondage and captivity for so long—whether it was with the porn industry, going through the court system, being in jail, or being on house arrest—and now it was almost all over.

Peyton decided we needed to go out and celebrate. When you are on house arrest, your restriction ends at a specific time; once it ends, you can leave the house. You still have the ankle bracelet on, and you don't get it off until the next day, but you are free to leave. My arrest ended at seven that night, so Peyton decided to take me to LA with her friends Judith and Mercy, to a theater where actors, directors, and models go to hear music and a Bible message.

The message was about being free from captivity (appropriate for me since I had just literally gotten off house arrest), and it was nice to be out and about. Afterward, we went to a place called BOA, a restaurant in LA. We had some sushi and I had a glass of wine. It was nice to just be able to sit outside and feel the fresh air. It was freeing, but also a little scary, because what was I supposed to do now? I couldn't live with Peyton forever, I couldn't work at On The Border forever. What should I do?

The next day, I got my ankle bracelet off and started to help Papa J in his ministry. Papa J would cook for weddings, and I would help him with his grandsons. This family had become like my own; Papa J was my grandpa, and I loved him dearly.

Eventually, Peyton told me I needed to find a place to live. She knew a woman by the name of Chin, who said that I could move into her house and pay rent. She also had a car that was her son's, which she said I could buy from her, so I moved in; not long after, Peyton's friend Judith moved in to rent another room.

Judith and I started to hang out, and we would go to LA a lot. I was always worried I would run into people from the porn industry, but we always went to places where celebrities were. Judith told me God gave her a ministry to celebrities. I hated celebrities, since there were a few who had bought and raped me, but even so I went with her because it was nice to have a friend—and it was doubly nice to be free to do what I wanted to.

Usually, we would go to places and I would run into a celebrity without even knowing who they were. I didn't want to minister to celebrities, and I really didn't even want to be around them. I didn't know who might, at any time, recognize me and try something inappropriate. I wasn't in physical captivity anymore, but I was still captive to the fear of who might to try to kidnap me, rape me, buy me, or sell me.

As Judith and I got closer, Chin became jealous. She didn't like us hanging out and became very hostile toward us. She also started dating this guy who, when he was around, gave me a creepy, eerie feeling. I hated when he spent the night, scared he was going to come in my room. In fact, one night, I saw someone come into my room. It was dark, and I heard, "I am going to get you…" I didn't know what it was, and still don't to this day, but I knew I needed to get out of that house. I had been around bad men before, and I felt that Chin's boyfriend was one of those bad men.

† † †

I had a friend at this time whom I haven't mentioned yet. I met him when I was married to Adrian and worked on a golf course as a cart girl. He was funny and handsome, and his name was Cole, and we became friends. He lived in Colorado, but his parents lived in California, so when he was in town visiting, we would hang out. I gave him my number and we managed to stay in contact over the years. Of course, there were years of gaps in our communication because of the porn industry, jail, cancer, and marriage.

One day I ended up calling him—I wasn't even sure if he had the same number—and he answered. His birthday was around the corner, and he asked me if I wanted to come to Colorado to visit. I was ecstatic, so I bought a ticket to Colorado. Cole and I had a lot of fun and a lot of laughs and, because this is what I did with men, we wound up sleeping together.

Nevertheless, I enjoyed the weekend and went home. As soon as I got home, though, Chin flew off the handle and kicked me and Judith out. Judith had expressed our concerns about Chin and her boyfriend to Peyton, and Chin didn't like it.

I called Peyton to let her know we'd been kicked out, and Peyton said I could come back to her house, but only temporarily. I understood. Peyton needed to have her life back. So I moved in with her, continued to work at On The Border, started to go to church at the Sanctuary every Sunday, and continued to help Papa J cook for weddings.

One day, out of nowhere, I felt really sick. I didn't know what was going on, but I decided to take a pregnancy test.

It was positive.

I started to freak out.

Great, I'm pregnant from a man that I really barely know. Even though I've been acquainted with him for ten years, I sure as heck don't know him well enough to have his baby.

I pulled myself together and called Cole to let him know the news, and he started yelling at me. He went crazy and then hung up. I thought, Here we go; I'm going to raise this baby all on my own.

Cole's friend Elliot lived in LA. He heard what was going on and called me and asked me to meet him for dinner. I agreed and met with him at a pizza place in Irvine, told him I was pregnant, and showed him the ultrasound pictures I'd gotten from my doctor's office. He called Cole.

"This is legit," he said. "She is pregnant."

"Tell him if I don't hear from him by Sunday, then I will raise this baby on my own," I said.

I went to church that Sunday and while I was in church Cole sent me a long text message—yeah, I said text—to tell me he wanted to raise this baby with me and wanted to step up and be a dad. So I called him later that day to talk about it.

"When are you moving to Colorado?" he asked.

"Wait," I said, "I'm not just going to pick up and move to Colorado."

We talked and talked and... I decided I would move with him so we could try to raise this baby together. He was going to visit California for the holidays, so we made a plan that, after Christmas, I would drive back to Colorado with him.

It was weird and awkward that I was about to move to another state with a man I barely knew, but I was prepared to do it.

Then we found out I was pregnant with twins—a boy and a girl. I was going to be responsible for two lives.

I spent the holidays with Peyton, her family, and Papa J, as well as with Cole and his family. We told Cole's parents I was pregnant. They were a little shocked since they didn't know me all that well, but they handled it pretty well.

After Christmas, it was time to go, so I said goodbye to Peyton, her kids, and to Papa J, and set off to start a new life.

† † †

I miscarried.

Shortly after we moved to Colorado, I lost the babies.

Cole and I were having a hard time, so I thought maybe I just needed to move back to California. I was trying to make it work with him, but it was hard because we didn't know each other and had both just suffered a horrible loss. We didn't love each other; we were just stuck together in an awkward circumstance.

Cole and I both were really bad at expressing our emotions, so we didn't communicate about how we felt throughout this crazy process.

After a few weeks, I got really sick for a few days. It got so bad that Cole took me to the hospital where they did some tests, including an ultrasound.

That's when the nurse came in and said, "You're pregnant."

Thirty seconds later the doctor came in and said, "Congratulations! Are you happy?"

I just lost two babies, I thought. I can't go through this again.

We went home that night and didn't talk. We just went to bed. The next day, we woke up to face our circumstances. The emergency room personnel had given me a list of obstetricians, and I found an awesome doctor who cared for me throughout my pregnancy. There were multiple factors that had led to me miscarrying the twins that didn't play into this pregnancy, so I carried to term and delivered a healthy son.

If I hadn't miscarried the twins, I wouldn't have my beautiful son today.

As for Cole and I: we just were not meant to be together. We only have one thing in common, and that's our son. I knew I needed to stand up on my own two feet, and so I got a job, got my own apartment, and started taking care of myself and my baby.

† † †

When I was still pregnant, I tried finding a church to go to. I couldn't find somewhere I connected with, until eventually I reached out to a pastor by the name of Craig Gross. When I lived with Peyton, I knew him as the "porn pastor." He worked with this ministry called XXXchurch. When I was still in porn, I would go to the adult film shows and see the signs that read Jesus Loves Porn Stars—I always thought they were kind of funny.

So when I moved to Colorado and was having a hard time finding a church, I remembered Craig and asked him if he had any suggestions for a church I could attend. He told me about one that was very close to my house, and I started going when my son was about three months old. I could go into the service when he was really little because he would just hang out in his car seat. When he started to become mobile, I would take him to a special room with seats and a video feed so I could still listen to the message while my son crawled around on the floor.

One Sunday, a pastor came up to me and introduced himself as Mason, the missions pastor. He didn't creep me out when he introduced himself; he actually had this sweet kind of spirit about him that made you want to tell him all your problems.

I did just that.

I told him I used to be in the adult film industry and how I heard about the church through the porn pastor, Craig Gross. Mason didn't even blink an eye, and he wasn't judgmental; he was just loving and kind to me. He really listened and made me feel like this church was my new home church. I think a part of me wanted to tell this pastor where I came from to test him and see how he would treat me in his church. He was sweet and welcomed me with open arms.

† † †

I would see Mason most Sundays, and he would always be sweet to my son. As my son got older and started running around, Mason would play and run around with him too.

Eventually, Mason introduced me to another pastor named Grayson and his wife, Zoe. Every time I would meet a pastor or their wife, my skepticism would be at an all-time high. Zoe was tall and beautiful, and when I met her I knew she wasn't your "typical" pastor's wife; I knew she had had life experiences in which people had hurt her, so we connected in an unspoken way. I felt the same connection with Mason's wife; there was a level of pain that she understood. When I first met Grayson, he was really tall and had no hair, so I immediately associated him with Pastor Henry—but once I spoke with him, I realized how stupid that was. He was the funny pastor, making light of the situation.

I started to build relationships with Zoe, Grayson, and Mason, opening up little by little about my story and what I had gone through. They would listen and just love me through it. I have to admit that sometimes, I would try to tell them something really shocking to get a reaction or to maybe test them a little to see— would they stick around as friends? Would they stick around at all? They did, and I never shocked them to the point where they ran away or abandoned me. They did what Peyton would do: simply listen and love me.

It was weird for me to be in a church that was safe, that wasn't trying to get anything out of me. As I opened up to them and told them my story, they suggested I go to counseling and told me the church would pay for it completely. At first, I wondered what they wanted in return; why would they pay for that? But then I began to realize they didn't want anything—they just wanted to love this broken porn star who didn't trust church or Jesus.

I started going to therapy on a weekly basis, and it was a very intense process. I had to relive what I had gone through, coming to terms with the truth that I was not at fault for a lot of the things that had happened. Yes, some of my choices were not the correct ones, but on the other hand, many other people in my life hadn't made the right choices regarding my life either.

My therapist told me I had a case of post-traumatic stress disorder, which I could see to be true. You don't get raped over and over for years and years and not have PTSD.

† † †

Today, I continue to go my church and, with the help of these pastors and their wives, I am able to write my story to help other women who have come from what I come from. Whether they've suffered abuse as a child, abuse in a relationship, abuse in the church, or abuse with sex, if I can help just one person, then putting my story on paper was worth it.

I can tell you that if you don't have faith in the church, I understand that. If you don't have faith in Jesus anymore—or never did—I understand that. I can tell you that I gave up believing, and then a porn pastor who said, "Jesus loves porn stars" referred me to a church that loves me and my son without condition. Believe me, there have been times when they have seen me flip out, seen things that "trigger" me and set me off, but this small group of leaders has stood by, and they haven't abandoned me. They have been with me through the process of writing this story. It took me over thirty years to find the right church; thirty years to find out who Jesus really is.

Awesome churches exist, awesome pastors exist, awesome pastors' wives exist. You just need to believe they are out there. I am living firsthand who Jesus really is; I see it in my church and I see it in my life.

The Jesus who was presented to me as a little girl from my father? He wasn't real.

The Jesus my mom told me about? He wasn't real.

The Jesus in the apostolic church? He wasn't real.

The Jesus Sophie told me about? He wasn't real.

The Jesus I felt in jail...

The Jesus I felt at Peyton's house...

The Jesus Papa J showed me...

The Jesus Luis and Polly showed me...

The Jesus at my church now...

The Jesus who lives in my heart now...

He is very much real.

You can read my story and see the real Jesus: the Jesus who loved drunks and prostitutes, the Jesus who turned water into wine, and the Jesus who loves porn stars is very much real. Even in your darkest place, there is an unconditional love. You just have to reach deep and believe Jesus is there. Faith as small as a mustard seed is all you need.

† † †

The pieces of my life and the people in my life were strategically put there by God.

Crystal Lewis sang "Come Just As You Are."

Peyton's sister is married to the man who wrote that song.

Peyton was supposed to be friends with my sister Sophie for a season, so she could come into my life and show me God's grace.

Papa J was supposed to be in my life and will always be in my heart.

Cole was supposed to be in my life because he is half of my beautiful, amazing son.

The church I attend now was supposed to be there to help me tell my story (not everyone else's versions of my story, but my story), to help me find my voice and show me there are legitimate churches in this world.

I have come across a lot of horrible people in my life. I was tortured and raped. I was in bondage for years, and now I have stepped up and am living a normal life. A "civilian" life.

One thing is for sure: what a normal life is for you is not a normal life for me. Sure, I get up every day and get dressed, get my son ready and go to work, come home and get my son dinner, give him a bath, put him to bed, and work on writing this book or my blog.

But what you don't see is me trying to act normal. Even going to a normal job every day is challenging. For years, my life consisted of other people selling my body so they could make money. Now I need to make my own money and take care of my family, but it's hard.

I work on not allowing things to set me off, because one word can make me lose it. One look, one touch. These are triggers for me. Some ordinary things I do can turn horrifying, like taking a shower and getting water on my face. I want to get baptized again, but I'm afraid that if I get into another huge tub of water and allow my pastor to baptize me, I will drown. I swore I would not allow anyone to have control of my body again, and allowing someone to baptize me gives them that control.

I also found out recently that Sophie and Charlotte started a organization to help girls involved in human trafficking. Peyton told me about it, and told me she had sent some of my blog—MyFathersDaughters—to Sophie. Sophie has now taken stories off my blog and tried to make them her own.

When their own sister was being trafficked, instead of trying to help me, they tried to sell me back or told me God would not forgive me. How do they expect to help someone else? I know there will come a day that God will bring me justice, and I know that he will not bless a ministry out of spite. I was the girl who was raped, I was beaten, I almost died, I went to jail, I was almost sold to a man overseas, and I was on house arrest.

And I was freed from captivity.

You may wonder why the last thing I decided to write about is my family. Well, my entire life I have had opposition. It started with my family, and I know that through this process of me telling my story, that opposition is going to continue with my family. I've had people use me as their pawn from the time I was a little girl until my thirties.

I rarely sleep well, because I have nightmares of the things that were done to me by my family and by many evil men and women in churches and in the porn industry. I'm always scared someone will find me. I'm scared my family will find me. I'm scared they will find my son. I'm scared of wanting to love again. I'm scared of wanting to have a relationship, because no man should have to take on my burdens. I'm scared that my son will grow up and hate me for the choices I have made. And I'm scared to move forward and publish this book because of all the horrible people in my life.

But...

I've turned my lack of sleep into my worship with God. If they find me, I will show them the love of Christ and I will also show them the fight I have now.

If my family finds me, I will simply tell them they are not welcome in my life, and I will also let them know that they are not to thank for my strength.

If they find my son, it will show them that their wrongs made them miss out on seeing one amazing kid grow up. God fixed my fear of loving again when he gave me my son, because my love for him, the unconditional love I have, is priceless.

If God wants to give me a relationship, then I believe he will bring me a man who will walk alongside me in all my craziness—and if God never does that, then Jesus is the best husband I can ask for.

And as far as my son hating me, I don't think that will ever happen. All I need to do is simply and purely love him.

As far as this book goes, I have decided that now is the time... I fasted for twenty-one days, broke the fast, and decided to send this book. The people who helped me with this process and who walked along this journey with me are some amazing people. The laypeople and leadership at my church are the ones to thank for this book. They are the ones to thank for showing me how real Jesus is in this season of my life.

† † †

I want to help people who have gone through what I have gone through. I want girls to know they don't have to sell their body to make a living. I am a living testimony. I can survive working a normal job and have somewhat a normal life—I just had to make the choice. I know you can't do it on your own, and if you're reading this book and are alone, then let me help... I know life will never be "normal," but it can only be as good as you allow it to be.

I know the feeling of wanting to die, but with that feeling I also found the feeling of wanting to live. Let me help you find that life again.

When I was on house arrest, I stopped and let Jesus speak to me; it took house arrest for me to hear Jesus' voice. What will it take for you to stop and listen? I am okay now knowing I was a broken vase. Jesus has glued me back together and now I am a little rough around the edges, but I am grateful—oh, so grateful—for those cracks, because without them Jesus wouldn't be my best friend today, and I wouldn't understand what grace meant. My choices are what took me to the porn industry, and it is my choices now that let me live a normal life, have a normal job, and be one kickass mommy.

God has been good to me. I know now without a shadow of a doubt Jesus was there, watching over me and protecting me. I am now on my journey to knowing what beauty truly is.

And... I am my Father's daughter.

Jeremiah 29:11-13

"For I know the plans that I have for you," declares the LORD, "plans for welfare and not for calamity to give you a future and a hope. Then you will call upon Me and come and pray to Me, and I will listen to you. And you will seek Me and find Me, when you search for Me with all your heart."

Psalm 9:9-10

"The LORD also will be a stronghold for the oppressed, a stronghold in times of trouble, and those who know Thy name will put their trust in Thee; for Thou, O LORD, hast not forsaken those who seek Thee."

My Fathers Daughter

CPSIA information can be obtained at www.ICGtesting.com
Printed in the USA
LVOW08s0815250614

391639LV00004B/293/P

9 780982 638255